A Thought For Today To Guide My Way

Published by forest-for-the-trees Publishing

DIGITAL PRODUCTIONS

barbara.tancredi@gmail.com

ISBN-13: 978-1468144536

ISBN-10: 1468144537

Manufactured in the United States of America

Dear Reader;

My prayer is that daily reading of these Christian truths will guide children to spiritual maturity.

Acknowledgements

To the Reverend Graham Jeffery my heartfelt thanks for his artistic talent so generously shared, his humor and for his cherished friendship. The Reverend Graham's contributions bring the pages to life.

To my daughter, Vera Joy Ferguson, I gratefully acknowledge her love and encouragement which inspired me to complete this book.

Dedication

Lovingly Dedicated

to

Christopher Ryan Horton

January 1

This is the day the Lord has made;
let us rejoice and be glad in it.
Psalm 118:24

Today is the first day of a brand new year. It is also the first day of January, the first month of the New Year. Can you find January 1 on the calendar?

Thought

I wonder what good things the New Year has in store?

January 2

In the beginning God created the heavens and the earth.

Genesis 1:1

What do you see when you look up into the sky? In the daytime you see clouds
or the sun with its bright light. At night you see the moon and stars.
Human hands made none of these things in the heavens.
Can you name some things outdoors that God made when
He created the earth?

Thought

I am glad for the trees, the hills and for all the
animals large and small.

This is the day

      the Lord has made

We will rejoice and be glad

      in it

January 3

Then God said, "Let us make man in our image, in our likeness."
Genesis 1:26

God created us to be a part of His family.
He is our loving heavenly Father.

Thought

I am God's beloved child.

January 4

Dear friend, I pray that you may enjoy good health.

3 John 2

God made our bodies strong and healthy.

When we get sick we soon feel well again.

Thought

Good food, exercise and rest keep my body healthy.

keep me fit.
Lord

wind me up

and set me
running

January 5

The earth is the Lord's, and everything in it, the world and those who live in it.

Psalms 24:1

This is my Father's world,
And to my listening ear
All nature sings, and 'round me rings
The music of the spheres.

This is my Father's world:
I rest me in the thought
Of rocks and trees, of skies and seas;
His hands the wonders wrought...
Hymn/Babcock

Thought

I am God's child alive in His wonderful world.

January 6

So God created man in His own image, in the image of God he created him; male and female he created them.

Genesis 1:27

The first people God made were Adam and Eve. He put them in a beautiful place called the Garden of Eden, where they often talked with God. In the middle of the garden was an apple tree. God told Adam and Eve they could eat any fruit they wanted, but they were not to eat of the apple tree.

Adam and Eve were in charge of all the animals God had created. One of the animals was a walking, talking snake. The snake spoke to Eve and said, "Go ahead, eat the apple. If you do, you will be as wise as God." Eve listened to the snake, picked an apple and gave a part of it to Adam. When God called out for them they were ashamed and hid themselves.

Because they had disobeyed God, Adam and Eve were turned out of the beautiful garden. And the snake's punishment was that he could no longer walk and talk, but had to crawl in the dust.

What was Adam and Eve's big mistake?

Thought

When I have a choice between right and wrong,
I will choose to do what is right.

January 7

If you obey my commandments, you will remain in my love, just as I have obeyed my Father's commands, and remain in his love.

John 15:10

As you grow day by day you are learning there is a right way to behave and a wrong way. You are learning that God expects us, His children, to do what is right.

SINAI

For best results, follow the Maker's instructions.

Thought
Father, lead me day by day,
Ever in Your perfect way.
Teach me to be pure and true,
Show me what I ought to do. Amen

January 8

(*God said*), "You shall have no other gods before me."
Exodus 20:3

The first commandment means that we are
not to love any person or thing
more than we love God. The God who
made us deserves to be first in our hearts.

Thought

I will love God with all my heart. I will do what He tells me to do.

January 9

(God said), **"You shall not make for yourself an idol, in the form of anything in heaven above or on the earth beneath or in the water below."**

Exodus 20:4

This second of God's commands means that we are not to worship anything that we can touch or see.
Only God is worthy to be worshipped.

Thought

I will give God first place in my heart.

January 10

You shall not misuse the name of the Lord your God, for the Lord will not hold anyone guiltless who misuses his name.

Exodus 20:7

God commands that His name be spoken with respect. His name is Holy.
God notices how we use His name.

If you keep shouting my name when you don't need me, How will I know when you do?

Thought

I will speak God's name with reverence.

January 11

Remember the Sabbath day by keeping it holy.

Exodus 20:8

We are commanded to keep Sundays holy. Many people rest from work on that day. Most Christians keep the day holy by going to worship services.

Thought

I will make Sunday
a day of rest and worship.

January 12

Honor your father and your mother.
Exodus 20:12

God is pleased with children who show honor and respect to parents. And parents of good children feel great delight. Foolish children ignore their parents' instructions. Children who do wrong cause parents great heartache.

Thought

I will obey my parents in all that is right.

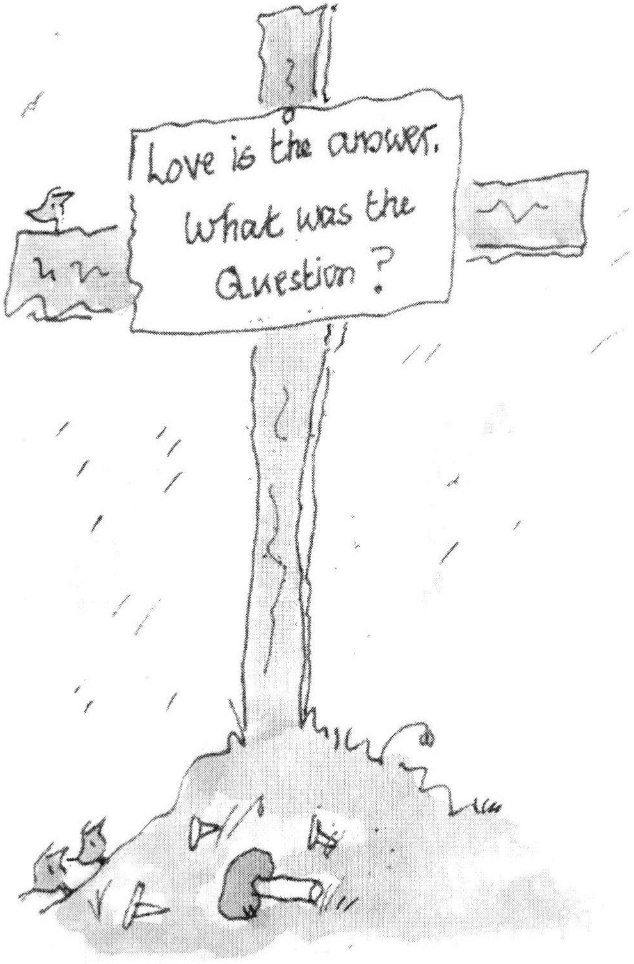
Love is the answer.
What was the
Question?

January 13

You shall not murder.

Exodus 20:13

God's sixth command is that we should not murder.
God's children should not like guns or anything that
could destroy another person.

Thought

I will show respect for
everyone's life.

January 14

You shall not commit adultery.

Exodus 20:14

God's seventh commandment is for
people who are married.
They are to keep their promise to
love each other always.

Thought

Forgiveness is a part of love.

January 15

You shall not steal.

Exodus 20:15

God's eighth command is clear. In plain words, if something isn't yours, then leave it alone. Nobody likes a thief. Many people are in prison for stealing.

Our world would be a happier place if everyone obeyed God's commands.

Thought
Stealing offends God and others.

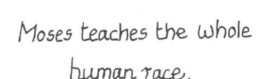

Moses teaches the whole human race.

January 16

(God said), "You shall not bear false testimony against your neighbor."
Exodus 20:16

This ninth commandment is about telling the truth.
God's children should speak the truth always.
If something is not true, refuse to say it.

Sometimes one may end up being punished
because of telling the truth.

Even so, it is more important to do as God says
and be truthful than it is to avoid punishment.

Thought
I want others to trust me, so I will be truthful.

January 17

You shall not covet.

Exodus 20:17

The tenth commandment is a warning to God's people that they are not to be envious or jealous of other people's things.
By being thankful for all we have, it's easier not to wish for what another person has.

Thought

"The world is so full of a number of things;
I'm sure we should be as happy as kings."

(R.L. Stevenson)

January 18

And he *(Jacob)* had a dream in which he saw a stairway resting on the earth, with its top reaching to heaven… and behold, a ladder was set on the earth with its top reaching to heaven.
Genesis 28:12

We celebrate the birthday of Dr. Martin Luther King. Dr. King was a black man. He had a dream that black and white people would live together in harmony. He was killed because of his dream, but his words will never die.

High
and
Low

Jesus loves the little children
All God's children of the world.
Red and yellow, black and white,
They are precious in His sight,
Jesus loves the little children of the world.
(Children's Hymn)

Rich and
poor

One with
another.

Thought
God loves everyone and so do I.

January 19

A longing realized is sweet to the soul.
Proverbs 13:19

A big wish, a big dream could be the beginning of a special goal.
One day when your goal is met you will say, "I finally did it!
I made my dream come true."

 the more I use my talent, the more it grows.

Thought

I will pray for God's guidance to help
me reach my goals.

January 20

**For everyone who has will be given more,
and he will have an abundance.**

Matthew 25:29

Use your talents and abilities however great or small to help others.
This is pleasing to God.

Thought
It makes me happy to use my talents and gifts to help others.

January 21

. . . the Son of Man did not come to be served, but to serve.

Matthew 20:28

When Jesus lived among us He went about helping and serving others by
healing, teaching and preaching. We all need help sometimes.

Can you think of someone who has helped you?

Pass on the good deed!

Be quick to help others.

Thought

I will help others cheerfully.

January 22

...if anything is excellent or praiseworthy – think about such things.
Philippians 4:8

On each video the library has a sticker that reads,
"Please Be Kind, Rewind."
It's a small polite thing to do, just pressing the
rewind button so that the next person can begin
the video easily.

Thought

I will look for ways to be kind and thoughtful today.

January 23

(Jesus said), "... **whoever wants to be great among you**
must be your servant."
Matthew 20:26

"Hey, look at me! Let me be first. Do it my way.
I'm the best. I win. You lose."
All of these attitudes are selfish ones.
When you learn to put others first,
you will be more like Jesus.

I didn't know there were any other Masters.

Thought

I will treat others as I would like to be treated.

January 24

**And he took the children in his arms, put his hands on them
and blessed them.**

Mark 10:14-16

Jesus loves me this I know
For the Bible tells me so.
Little ones to Him belong.
They are weak, but He is strong
–Anna B. Warner–

No strength but
YOURS'

Thought

What a friend I have in Jesus!

January 25

Everyone who heard him was amazed at his understanding and his answers.

Luke 2:47

Jesus was once a child just as you are. At an early age He learned all about God's commandments. One day He went with his parents to the temple in Jerusalem. While there he listened to the teachers and asked them questions.

Thought

I listen and ask questions
so that I may learn.

and most of them at Nazareth

January 26

For God will bring every deed into judgment, including every hidden thing, whether it is good or evil.

Ecclesiastes 12:14

Those who choose to do wrong often think that God has not noticed them because they seem to go unpunished. Not true. Every sin is punished and every good deed is rewarded – if not in this life, they will be rewarded or punished in the life to come.

I kept my talent under the bed

Thought

Nothing I do or say is hidden from God.

January 27

"Come, follow me," Jesus said, "and I will make you fishers of men."

Matthew 4:19

Many Christian people put a small fish on their automobiles. The fish is a symbol of the Christian faith. When Jesus called the fishermen – Peter, James, and John – to be His followers, He told them, "Follow me and I will make you fishers of men."

Thought

The fish symbol reminds me of Jesus' followers.

January 28

Even a child is known by his actions,
by whether his conduct is pure and right.
Proverbs 20:11

When you do what is pure and good, when you do your best;
know that God in heaven approves
and your acts will be blessed.

with a life like mine
who needs a sermon?

Thought

I want to be like Jesus.

January 29

**In all your ways acknowledge him, and he will make
your paths straight.**

Proverbs 3:6

God's formula for success is that we admit
our dependence on Him and ask His help.
With God's help, how can we fail?

*The Lord himself
stands beside
me. Therefore
I cannot be
afraid.*

Thought

God will help me when
I ask Him.

January 30

For this is what the Soverign Lord says,
"I Myself will search for my sheep and look after them."
Ezekiel 34:11

Your pet trusts and expects you to give loving care.
Who will pour Rover's chow? Who will change Tabby's litter?
Who will take good care of the delightful little critter?

Thought

My pet depends on me, and I depend on Jesus.

January 31

He who walks with the wise grows wise. . .
Proverbs 13:20

Learn from your parents, grandparents, and teachers too.

They are older and wiser and have much to teach you.

Thought
I will become wiser today by listening to my
parents and teachers.

February 1

My times are in your hands.

Psalms 31:15

Today begins the shortest month of the year—February.

Enjoy each and every day. Try not to waste time.

It's the stuff life is made of.

Hello World.

Thought

Thank you, God, for this new
month and this new day.

February 2

**And Jesus grew in wisdom and stature, and in favor
with God and men.**

Luke 2:52

God gave each of us a body, mind and spirit. The spirit part,
the way we feel and think, lives forever. God expects us to
take care of our bodies, our minds, and our spirits.
How will you take care of your body today? Your mind?
Your spirit?

bought WITH A PRICE

Thought

I will take good care of myself today.

February 3

Remember your Creator in the days of your youth.

Ecclesiastes 12:1

Who can make the sunshine?

I'm sure I can't; can you?

Oh, who can make the sunshine?

No one but God, it's true.

(Children's Hymn)

Thought

Thank You Father for the sunshine after the rain. Amen

February 4

Blessed is the man who perseveres under trial.

James 1:12

If you don't get it right the first time, keep trying again and again. Some things that are hard for you to learn may be easy for your friend. Be glad when your friends succeed, and be thankful for the many things you are able to do.

Thought

I will not give up easily.

February 5

...for God loves a cheerful giver.

2 Corinthians 9:7

The Bible teaches us to be kind and helpful to others. When asked to help, do it cheerfully without complaining. God blesses a cheerful helper.

Thought

One, two buckle my shoe.

Three, four shut the door.

Five, six pick up sticks.

Seven eight shut the gate.

Whatever job I'm asked to do,

I'll happily do my best for you.

February 6

For I am the Lord, your God, who takes hold of your right hand and says to you, Do not fear, I will help you.

Isaiah 41:13

When you feel afraid, imagine your hand in God's hand and refuse to worry. God is in charge and He loves you.

My hand in Your's, Lord.

Thought

Instead of being afraid I will trust God.

February 7

Dear children, let us not love with words or tongue, but with actions and in truth.

1 John 3:18

It's not enough to say, "I love you."
I have to show I care.
I show by deeds of kindness,
I show love when I share.

Thought

I will show love today to those I meet.

February 8

Freely you have received, freely give.

Matthew 10:8

"What do I have to give small as I am?" you might wonder. You might think you have nothing to give, but anytime you give a smile or a kind word your gift is big and beautiful in God's sight.

Thought

Lord, thank You for the joy of giving and that I have plenty of love to give away.
Amen

February 9

Your word is a lamp to my feet and a light to my path.
Psalms 119:105

The Bible is called God's word because it was God Himself who told the writers what to write. God tells us about the beginning of the world in Genesis and about how the world will end in the last book, Revelation. The Bible also tells us about Jesus who showed us how to live happy lives.

Thought

Dear God, thank You for Your book, the Bible. Bless me as I read, study and listen to its words. Amen

February 10

Come to me, all you who are weary and burdened, and I will give you rest.

Matthew 11:28

Do you have a quiet time during your busy day? In Mexico they call their quiet time a siesta. Many grown-ups and children have a mid-day naptime. During your quiet time, remember that God's thoughts sometime come to us when we are waiting and still.

Thought

In my quiet time I will think about God.

February 11

There are six things which the Lord hates, seven which are detestable to him.

Proverbs 6:16

God tells us clearly in the Bible what kind of behavior He hates.
God is not pleased when we act unfriendly or say things that are untrue.
When there is fighting in families God's heart is sad.

Thought

Lord, keep me far from doing
anything that You hate.

February 12

It is good to praise the Lord.

Psalm 92:1

Have you ever done something really nice for a friend
and that person forgot to even say "thank you?"
How did it make you feel? Well, that is just how God
feels when He answers our prayers and we forget to say
"Thank You" to Him.

Thought

I will not forget to give thanks.

February 13

**Nobody should seek his own good, but the
good of others.**

1 Corinthians 10:24

Nobody has to tell you what you need or want. You know very well these things. Many times it's others who help us get what we are longing for. God often answers our prayers by sending just the right person to help us.

Thought

I will be mindful of the needs of others.

February 14

(Jesus said) "By this all men will know that you are my disciples, if you love one another."

John 13:35

Happy Valentine's Day! Each valentine you give and receive is a way to show friendship and love. Can you draw a Valentine heart? It is a picture or symbol of love.

Thought

God is love.

February 15

. . .The Lord does not look at the things man looks at. Man looks at the outward appearance, but the Lord looks at the heart.

1 Samuel 16:7

Yesterday you drew a picture of a heart. Can you find a picture in a book or a magazine that pictures love in action? It might be a Mother caring for her baby, or a child feeding a pet, or a Father pushing a child in a swing. Look for love.

It's all around you.

Thought

If I look for love I will find it.

February 16

Delight yourself in the Lord and he will give you the desires of your heart.

Psalms 37:4

to see

to hear

to Love

to serve

Lord, open my eyes to see You.

Lord, open my ears to hear You.

Lord, open my heart to love You.

Lord, open my hands to serve You.

Thought
God is everywhere.

February 17

**Then you will call upon me and come and pray to me, and
I will listen to you.**

Jeremiah 29:12

Praying before meals, at bedtime, and in church are times when
most people pray. God is always listening anytime we send a silent
thought to Him. He waits for you to ask Him for His help.

Thought

Thank you, God, for listening to and
answering my prayers. Amen

February 18

The Lord knows the thoughts of man...
Psalms 94:11

Do you realize that you are in control of your thoughts? You can choose to see the best in others. You can even choose to be cheerful when you feel like whining. And you can choose to be thankful instead of complaining.

but I always
see the best
in
You.

Thought

Lord, may my thoughts please You today. Amen

February 19

**The people all responded together,
'We will do everything the Lord has said.'**
Exodus 19:8

How many of the Ten Commandments can you remember? Listen to them again (Exodus 20). They are God's important rules for living.

Thought
Lord, keep me obedient to Your commands. Amen

February 20

**Now God had caused the official to show favor
and sympathy to Daniel.**

Daniel 1:9

If you have a Bible storybook, find the story about Daniel.

What do you notice that is special about Daniel?

How can you be like Daniel?

Dare to stand alone

DARE TO
be a
DANIELLA.
—
LION'S
DEN →

GRRRH

Thought

Daniel refused to serve anyone but God.

February 21

Be devoted to one another in brotherly love.

Romans 12:10

A wise person once said, "If you'd like to have a friend, be one."
Treat your friend as you want to be treated. Have fun and enjoy your
friends. They are special gifts from God.

Thought

I'm glad for my friends.

February 22

Show proper respect to everyone.

1 Peter 2:17

Each person you know deserves your respect.

Offer an older person your seat if it's needed.

Be glad to share things with others.

Thought

I will treat others just as I would like to be treated.

February 23

May the words of my mouth and the meditation of my heart be pleasing in your sight, O Lord, my Rock and my Redeemer.

Psalms 19:14

Today you will have many things to say.
Make sure your words help rather than hurt others.

Thought

Words have power.
They can bless or hurt.

February 24

And now these three remain: faith, hope and love.

But the greatest of these is love.

1 Corinthians 13:13

There is an old song that goes, "The best things in life are free."

Can you name some of these best things?

Remember, money can't buy love, joy, and happiness.

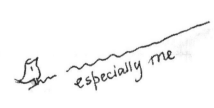

Thought

Thank You, God, for all the gifts
You freely give. Amen

February 25

(Jesus said) "In my Father's house are many rooms; if it were not so, I would have told you. I am going there to prepare a place for you."

John 14:2

At the end of a busy day it's great to be home. We like to be with our family and the things we love. Jesus told us that He is preparing a home for us in heaven someday. His blessings never end.

Bless O Lord,
this house
we pray
Keep it safe by night and day.

Thought

Thank You, Lord for my home and family here on earth and the one that You are preparing for me in heaven. Amen

February 26

You are observing special days and months and seasons and years!

Galatians 4:10

Can you name some things you especially enjoy about winter, the cold time of year? Think of the warmth of a cozy fire, hot chocolate, steaming soup, and warm blankets—just to name a few.

Thought

Spring, summer, winter, fall

By His mighty hand He made them all.

February 27

There is a time for everything...

Ecclesiastes 3:1

It doesn't matter what speed you go, so long as it's in the right direction.

The faster I hurry
The slower I get.
Best I not worry,
Best I not fret,
Time be my friend
From beginning to end.

Thought

My time is a gift from God.

February 28

"I am the Alpha and the Omega," says the Lord God, "Who is, and who was, and who is to come, the Almighty."

Revelation 1:8

February is coming to a close. Winter is ending.

With each ending there is a beginning.

We always have something new in store.

Thought

God gives us new beginnings.

See you tomorrow

February 29

**Devote yourselves to prayer, being watchful
and thankful.**

Colossians 4:2

Our prayers are not always answered immediately.
Our work is to keep on praying,
watching and expecting.
We have to learn to wait
and not give up.

Thought

God hears every prayer.

March 1

(Jesus answered) "The wind blows wherever it pleases. You hear its sound, but you cannot tell where it comes from and where it is going. So it is with everyone born of the Spirit."

John 3:8

You can't see the wind
Yet you know it's there.
You can feel it blow your hair.
You can't see the breeze
Move the leaves in the trees,
As it lifts your kite high,
As it soars into the sky.
You cannot see God,
Yet you know He is there.
Everyday He gives
You His loving care.

Janelle S. Larsen

I feel the wind, the wind feels me.

Thought

God's presence is everywhere.

March 2

(Jesus said) "I have told you that my joy may be in you and that your joy may be complete."

John 15:11

It's fun to surprise others and it's fun to be surprised. Can you think of a way to surprise someone you love? It might be a telephone call to a grandparent or it might be picking up your toys without being asked.

Thought

Every day is full of happy surprises.

March 3

Seek the Lord while he may be found; call upon him while he is near.

Isaiah 55:6

While my friend and I took a stroll near a golf course, I looked for stray golf balls. I usually found several, but my friend never found one. Why? She simply wasn't looking for them.

Is there anybody there?

Thought

If I seek I will find.

March 4

**They were terrified and asked each other, "Who then is this?
Even the wind and waves obey him!"**

Mark 4:41

Look out your window today and see if the wind is blowing. The wind that
we cannot see does many good things in our world. It blows away the dead
leaves, cleans our air, and is used to make electricity.

a good day for the
wind, a bad day
for fishing

Thought

The blowing March wind reminds me of God's Spirit that I feel but cannot see.

March 5

An angel from heaven appeared to him and strengthened him.
Luke 22:43

The Bible tells us a lot about angels. They live in heaven but sometimes come to earth as God's messengers. Angels announced Jesus' birth in Bethlehem. In Matthew 18:10, Jesus says that children have guardian angels in heaven.

This property is protected by Guardian Angels. Inc.

Thought

Sometimes angels come to earth as a person with no wings.

March 6

You will pray to him, and he will hear you, and you will fulfill your vows.

Job 22:27

Our Father who is in heaven,

May Your name be holy,

May Your kingdom come

On earth as it is in heaven.

Give us our daily bread.

Forgive us our wrongs

As we forgive others their wrongs against us.

May we not do evil.

Your kingdom, Your power, and Your glory are

forever and ever. Amen

we pray

our father

Thought

Prayer is the pathway to God.

March 7

He is like a tree planted by streams of water, which yields its fruit in season and whose leaf does not wither. Whatever he does prospers.

Psalm 1:3

An apple tree grows apples, a lemon tree grows lemons. We know what kind of tree it is by the fruit it grows. And when it comes to people, we know what kind of people they are by the fruits of their actions.

Do they show the bad fruits of lying, fighting, and laziness?

Or are they truthful, kind, cheerful,

and hard working?

Thought

A good person lives God's way.

March 8

In him our hearts rejoice, for we trust in his holy name.

Psalm 33:21

God who touches earth with beauty,

You can make my heart like new,

Keep me by Your Spirit

Pure and strong, and true.

Thought

God is leading me day by day.

March 9

Rejoice in the Lord, you who are righteous, and praise his holy name

Psalm 97:12

Do you enjoy dressing yourself and choosing
what you will wear each day?
Don't forget to put on a happy face
every morning.
It makes the day brighter for everyone.

Which one shall I wear today?

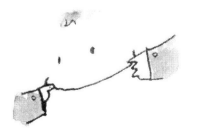

Thought

I can always find a reason to smile.

March 10

Be kind and compassionate to one another, forgiving each other, just as in Christ God forgave you

Ephesians 4:32

Sometimes you may feel more like getting even than forgiving someone who has made you angry... Forgiving others is easier if you remember the times you've needed to be forgiven. God forgives you if you are willing to forgive others.

If this is hard for you, ask for God's help.

Super-Glue is better than 'Blame U'!

You mend what is broken and make us better

Thought

I will ask God to help me forgive and forget.

March 11

**Who can proclaim the mighty acts of the Lord, or
fully declare his praise?**

Psalm 106:2

You are growing in faith and wisdom as you learn to know, love, and serve God.

Thought

My God is an awesome God.

In my own way, even I am a miracle

March 12

**Since my youth, O God, you have taught me, and to this day
I declare your marvelous deeds.**

Psalm 71:17

Look out your window and see if you can see any signs of spring.

One of the first spring flowers to bloom is the crocus.

Be on the lookout for spring flowers and birds and new growth on trees.

blossom where
you are planted

Thought

God provides the
miracle of spring.

I'm
here

We all in our own way
give God the glory

March 13

I guide you in the way of wisdom and lead you along straight paths.

Proverbs 4:11

The opposite of wise is foolish.

A foolish person pays no attention to what is right or wrong.

The wise person is always careful to do the right thing.

Thought

I'd rather be wise than foolish.

March 14

When a man's ways are pleasing to the Lord, he makes even his enemies live at peace with him.

Proverbs 16:7

Someone has hurt your feelings. You were not invited to play. Everyone knows what it's like to feel hurt or left out. You may be tempted to get even with the person who has hurt you. Instead, act friendly and loving. It's possible that your enemy may become your friend.

FOLLY

WISDOM

It's not always easy to read these sign-posts

Thought

Getting even gets me nowhere.

March 15

God, who has called you into fellowship with his Son Jesus Christ our Lord, is faithful.

1 Corinthians 1:9

Have you heard the story of Noah,
the ark, and the flood? (Genesis 6)
After the flood, God gave a beautiful rainbow as a sign that He would never
again destroy the world with a flood.

Thought

Rainbows remind me of God's promise.

March 16

For God so loved the world that he gave his one and only Son, that whoever believes in him should not perish but have eternal life.

John 3:16

One of God's great promises is that we will live forever in heaven with Him if we believe in Jesus Christ and live the way He taught.

I still think we should have waited for Noah.

Thought

My soul will live forever.

March 17

I rejoiced with those who said to me,
"Let us go into the house of the Lord."
Psalm 122:1

The church is called God's house.
It is where we go to worship and learn about
Him. Enter the church quietly and respectfully.
It is a place for prayer and praise.

I was glad when they said to me

'Let us come to your house, o God.'

Thought

I love to visit God's house.

March 18

For this reason I kneel before the Father, from whom his whole family in heaven and on earth derives its name.

Ephesians 3:14-15

Jesus of Nazareth lived here

And shall do again ... and and again.

All over the world people live in families. It is God's plan for us. Good parents and grandparents are special blessings.

Thought

I will pray for God to bless my family today.

March 19

Love is patient, love is kind. It does not envy, it does not boast, it is not proud.

1 Corinthians 13:4

What does it mean to have patience?

The patient person waits cheerfully.

When we are patient we show love to others.

Today you may need to be patient. Can you wait cheerfully?

Love has its own song

Thought

I will not lose my patience today.

March 20

Rejoice in the Lord always; I will say it again: Rejoice!

Philippians 4:4

Do you have a favorite song you like to sing?
Sing as you go about your work and play.

It's a good way to show the Lord that
you are full of joy.

God loves to hear his
crows as
well
as
his
nightingales

Thought

I will keep a song in my heart.

March 21

Then he took his staff in his hand, chose five smooth stones from the stream, put them in the pouch of his shepherd's bag and, with his sling in his hand, approached the Philistine.

1 Samuel 17:40

David faced the giant shouting, "This day the Lord of hosts will deliver you up into my hands!"
While the crowd watched, David aimed his slingshot and hit Goliath right between the eyes. The giant fell to the ground dead. David's people cheered and cheered and he became their hero.

Was there anything you wanted to say to me, Sonny?

One minute whilel fix this sling, Goliath.

Thought
Children can be heroes for God.

March 22

It is I who made the earth and created mankind upon it. My own hands stretched out the heavens; I marshaled their starry hosts.
Isaiah 45:12

God our Creator loves for you and me to be creative just as He is.
Can you draw a picture of a beautiful rainbow or a field of flowers?

Creating something new and
beautiful is fun and makes us happy.

I need to look at the sky before
I can paint it

Thought

God is creative and so am I.

March 23

By standing firm you will gain life.

Luke 21:19

When something seems too hard for you and you are ready to say
"I can't;" stop and think about *The Little Engine That Could.*
Tell yourself, "I think I can, I think I can."

Keep huffing and puffing and you'll
succeed too.

Thought

If it's going to be, it's up to me.

March 24

May God be gracious to us and bless us and make his face shine upon us...

Psalm 67:1

What will this day bring?
Each day has its special kind of magic.
Expect something wonderful to
happen today. It's your day to enjoy.

Some things talk
by just shining

Thought

God's blessings are new every day.

March 25

The apostles performed many miraculous signs and wonders among the people.

Acts 5:12

When Jesus lived on the earth He did many miracles. The Bible tells us about thirty-five of these miracles. Jesus turned water into wine, caused the disabled to walk, gave a blind man his sight, and brought Lazarus back from the dead.

In prayer we can ask God for a miracle and trust that He will give us His blessing and sometimes even a miracle, if that is what is best for us.

If Lazarus can do it, so can we.

Thought

I am thankful for all the blessings and miracles that God sends.

March 26

For God will bring every deed into judgment, including every hidden thing, whether it is good or evil.
Ecclesiastes 12:14

Do you know anyone who is blind, disabled or cannot hear well? Even with health challenges these special people are happy, enjoy friendship, the warm sunshine, laughter, good food, and other blessings that God gives us all.

Thought

I will befriend those who need me.

March 27

Wise men store up knowledge,...

Proverbs 10:14

George Washington Carver prayed to God that he might be shown the mysteries of the world. Instead God led him to explore the mysteries of a peanut. Over time he discovered hundreds of uses for the peanut and became famous.

Thought

Knowledge comes from God.

March 28

The name of the Lord is a strong tower; the righteous run to it and are safe.

Proverbs 18:10

Whatever work I'm asked to do
God gives me His help to see me through.
God helps the weak, God helps the small,
God helps me when I call.

Thought

I can depend on God.

God helps the great

he loves the small

March 29

**So we say with confidence, "The Lord is my helper;
I will not be afraid. What can man do to me?"**
Hebrews 13:6

When you need help ask God to help you. He loves you and is glad when you call on him. If you see someone who needs your help, do what you can to help that person.

Thought

He has no hands but my hands to do
His work today. He has no feet but
my feet to help someone on his way.

March 30

May your father and mother be glad;
may she who gave you birth rejoice!
Proverbs 23:25

Parents want the best for their children. When a child
is growing strong physically, mentally and spiritually
parents feel great joy and delight.
Good children are rewards that God gives parents.

Thought

I will make my parents proud of me.

March 31

The earth is the Lord's, and everything in it;
the world, and all who live in it.

Psalm 24:1

We're glad for springtime, so full of breezes, sunshine and showers. We look forward to Easter and the celebration of Christ's victory over death.

New life makes us glad—baby birds in their nests, spring flowers beginning to bud, and the world so alive and new.

And the little bird will rest in my branches

Thought
God gives new life.

April 1

The fool says in his heart, "There is no God."
Psalm 14:1

Today is April 1st, April Fool's Day. On this day we often play jokes on friends and family members. You might say, "I see a spider crawling in your hair!" If the person believes you, you can laugh and say, "April Fools".

Do not be quick to believe all that you are told on April Fools or any day. You, too, might be an April Fool.

But if You don't exist, what chance have we got?

Thought
I will ask myself, "Is this true; is this right?"

April 2

"...but whoever listens to me shall live in safety and be at ease, without fear of harm."

Proverbs 1:33

All of us have times when we are afraid or frightened. At scary times we want to be with someone who can comfort and protect us.

Parents do their best to comfort and protect.

Be thankful, too, for policemen, security guards, soldiers and sailors.

They help keep our world safe.

Thought

I feel safe and secure.

April 3

**To one he gave five talents of money, to another two talents,
and to another one talent, each according to his ability.
Then he went on his journey.**

Matthew 25:15

Are you good at drawing, acting, ball games,
singing or dancing? Whatever it is that you do well
is your talent. Talents come from God.
Your talents are for you to enjoy and develop,
and for others enjoyment.

I use my talent to the full.

Thought
I will make good use of my talents.

April 4

**Even a child is known by his actions, by whether his conduct
is pure and right.**

Proverbs 20:11

How you act or behave tells everyone what kind of person you are becoming.
Children who behave well and listen to the teachings of their parents
are a joy to be with.

Thought

My conduct says a lot about
me to others.

The smile you send out returns to you

April 5

Dear friends, since God so loved us, we also ought to love one another.

1 John 4:11

Your hand in mine, your good words and your smiles do a lot to make my world worthwhile.

All of us together, or only you and I – a happy song of friendship, a word or two of cheer, makes all the world much gladder just because my friend is near.

A friend is nice to be with.

Thought

A friend is nice to be with.

April 6

The land produced vegetation: plants bearing seed according to their kinds and trees bearing fruit with seed in it according to their kind. And God saw that it was good.

Genesis 1:12

Mary, Mary quite contrary, how does your garden grow? A garden grows best in good soil, with plenty of sunshine and the proper amount of water.

We do the planting and the watering, but it's God who makes things grow.

Thought
I am sowing seeds of kindness in my garden to make the world a happier place.

April 7

Keep you tongue from evil, and your lips from speaking lies.
Psalm 34:13

Do you know what it means to gossip?
Gossip is saying unkind things about one person to another.

With something as small as our tongues we can deeply hurt another person.

It's far better to say nothing than to say something hurtful.

Thought

I will keep my words kind today.

April 8

How can a young man keep his way pure?
By living according to your word.

Psalm 119:9

Our character is our true self, the way we behave when nobody is looking.

Every time you do what is right you are building good character, pleasing in God's sight.

True wisdom lies in knowing which way to go ...

Ohio *LONDON* *UTAH*

Thought

Good choices build good character.

April 9

Praise the Lord. Sing to the Lord a new song, his praise in the assembly of the saints.

Psalm 149:1

I'm inright, outright, downright
Happy all the time.
Since Jesus lives within
To keep my heart from sin,
I'm inright, outright, downright
Happy all the time.
(Children's Hymn)

It's the way we live our life

Thought

The world is a happy place.

April 10

**I will praise you as long as I live, and in your name
I will lift up my hands.**

Psalm 63:4

Count your blessings
Name them one by one.
Count your many blessings
See what God has done.

rejoice and be glad

Thought

My blessings are too many to count.

April 11

No discipline seems pleasant at the time, but painful. Later on, however, it produces a harvest of righteousness and peace for those who have been trained by it.

Hebrews 12:11

Be glad when someone shows you a better way.
Would you like to play a musical instrument, be a choir member or ride a bicycle?
Be willing to practice, practice, practice to learn to do anything well.

Thought
Practice helps me to learn something new.

April 12

Do not boast about tomorrow, for you do not know what a day may bring forth.

Proverbs 27:1

Today's a new day.
What kind will it be?
The mood of the day
Depends on me.
I can't change the weather,
Or what may happen—it's true;
But it's up to me whether
I'll be happy or blue.

I just LOVE my world

Thought
I will make this a good day.

April 13

Cast all your anxiety on him because he cares for you.
1 Peter 5:7

Sometimes people wonder why God allows bad things to happen. It is not for us to understand all of God's ways, but to know that He loves us and that we can trust in His love no matter what happens.

Thought

God will have the last word and
it will be good.

April 14

Whoever loves his brother lives in the light, and there is nothing in him to make him stumble.

1 John 2:10

When Jack and Jill trudged up the mound
To fetch a pail of water,
Poor Jill fell down and hit the ground
But Jack was there to help her.

Thought
A friend who helps when there is a need is a very good friend indeed.

April 15

The greatest among you will be your servant.
Matthew 23:11

Some of Jesus disciples or followers wanted a high office in His heavenly kingdom. Jesus surprised them by saying,
"If you want to be great you must be willing to serve others."
Jesus even washed His disciples feet to show them
an example of service.

Thought

I am willing to serve as
Jesus did.

April 16

The Lord detests lying lips, but he delights in men who are truthful.
Proverbs 12:22

In Proverbs 12:22 the Bible says plainly that we must tell the truth and keep our promises if we want to please God.

Thought

Honesty is the best policy.

April 17

By the seventh day God had finished the work he had been doing; so on the seventh day he rested from all his work.

Genesis 2:2

"All work and no play makes Jack a dull boy." Whether we are young or old, everyone needs time to play as well as work. Work when it's time to work and play when it's time to play. This is part of God's plan for us.

Thought

The best day is a balanced day of work and play.

April 18

Land that drinks in the rain often falling on it and that produces a crop useful to those for whom it is farmed receives the blessing of God.

Hebrews 6:7

On a rainy day you may feel like saying, "Rain, rain go away, Come again another day." God sends the rain because He knows rain is needed as well as sunshine in our world.

Jesus can do miracles even when its raining.

Thought

All sunshine makes a desert.

April 19

O Lord, hear my prayer, listen to my cry for mercy; in your faithfulness and righteousness come to my relief.

Psalm 143:1

God did not promise
Skies always blue
Flowers on our pathways
All our life through.
God did not promise
Sun without rain,
Joy without sorrow,
Peace without pain.

But God has promised
Strength for the day,
Rest for the labor,
Light for the way.
Help in our trials,
Aid from above,
Unfailing sympathy,
Undying love.

–Annie J. Flint

Thought
I can trust God to give what is best.

April 20

And whenever you stand praying, if you hold anything against anyone, forgive him, so that your Father in heaven may forgive you your sins.

Mark 11:25

Why is it important to forgive those who have hurt you?
It is natural to feel an urge to hurt back or get even.
You ask, "Do I have to forgive?"
God's word comes through loud and clear,
"You must forgive others if you
wish Me to forgive you."

Is it all right if I don't forgive cats?

I'm forgiving you whether you like it or not.

Thought

I need God's help to
truly forgive.

April 21

"They will also answer, 'Lord, when did we see you hungry or thirsty
or a stranger or needing clothes or sick or in prison,
and did not help you?'
"He will reply, 'I tell you the truth, whatever you did not do for one
of the least of these, you did not do for me.'

Matthew 25:44-45

When I help those in need,
I am doing it for Jesus, too.

Thought

I will help those in need
whenever I can.

April 22

The fear of the Lord is the beginning of knowledge, but fools despise wisdom and discipline.

Proverbs 1:7

Much wisdom may be found in the book of Proverbs in the Bible.

Knowledge is good but wisdom is even better. The good news is that God will give us wisdom if we ask Him for it and seek it.

Thought

Trusting God is the first step in becoming wise.

April 23

Give, and it will be given to you. A good measure, pressed down, shaken together and running over, will be poured into you lap. For with the measure you use, it will be measured to you.

Luke 6:38

The more we give away, the more we receive. God tells us to freely give to others. When we do, we will be surprised by God's blessings.

Thought
To love is to give.

April 24

**When Jesus spoke again to the people, he said,
"I am the light of the world. Whoever follows me will never walk in
darkness, but shall have the light of life."**

John 8:12

Jesus' teachings light up our pathway to heaven.

Thought

Jesus is the light of the world.

It's better to light one candle
than curse the darkness

April 25

Be devoted to one another in brotherly love. Honor one another above yourselves.

Romans 12:10

Help us to help each other, Lord.

May we lift our brother's care;

Not for gain or rich reward,

But for Christ's love to share.

Thought

I have lots of love to share.

April 26

God is our refuge and strength, a ever-present help in trouble.

Psalm 46:1

What a friend we have in Jesus!
He hears and answers our
prayers. He helps us whenever
we ask Him.
He never leaves us.

doesn't matter what speed you go, so long as it's in the right direction.

Jerusalem

Thought

God gives me confidence.

April 27

But a poor widow came and put in two very small copper coins, worth only a fraction of a penny. Calling his disciples to him, Jesus said, "I tell you the truth, this poor widow has put more into the treasury than all the others. They gave out of their wealth; but she, out of her poverty, put in everything -- all she had to live on."

Mark 12 42-44

Is your gift a big one or a small one? The size of the gift you have to give is not as important as how much love is put into the choosing. The smallest gift that is given with great love is a blessing to the giver and to the person who receives it.

   +

Thought
The Lord sees my heart.

April 28

After Job had prayed for his friends, the Lord made him prosperous again and gave him twice as much as he had before"

Job 42:10

In the Old Testament we can read the story about a good man whose name was Job. God allowed many troubles to come to Job as a test.
God wanted to know if Job would love and serve Him even though he had great sufferings.

PRAY FOR
ONE ANOTHER

Poor Job lost his family, his money, his health and his friends. Still, Job kept on loving and serving God. Job's great reward was that God gave him back double all that he had lost.

Thought
Job's righteousness was pleasing to God.

April 29

"For I did not speak of my own accord, but the Father who sent me commanded me what to say and how to say it."

John 12:49

Jesus speak and make me ready
When Your voice is plainly heard,
With a heart glad and steady
I will follow every word.
I am listening, Lord, for Thee.
Master, speak! O speak to me!

(Anonymous)

Thought
When He speaks I will listen.

April 30

Anyone who does wrong will be repaid for his wrong.
And there is no favoritism.

Colossians 3:25

In other words, God has no favorites. Remember David who killed the giant? God gave him special blessings and favor. But when David gave in to temptation by committing the sin of murder because of beautiful Bathsheba, David had to suffer for this sin. God did not allow David to build His holy temple in Jerusalem.

Thought
Wrong acts have serious consequences.

May 1

Shout with joy to God, all the earth! Sing the glory of his name; make his praise glorious!

Psalm 66:1-2

Sing along with the cheerful birds
a song of gladness for sunshine
and spring flowers.

Thought

All things bright and beautiful,
All creatures great and small,
All things wise and wonderful
The Lord God made them all.

(C. Alexander)

May 2

And Jesus grew in wisdom and stature, and in favor with God and men.

Luke 2:52

Respectful behavior shows that you are growing in wisdom. First honor and serve God with respect. And, because you are God's child, treat yourself with respect.

As you expect others to show respect to you, so you must act respectfully toward others.

I build on you as the waves rise higher

Jesus

Help me to build my life on you, Lord

Thought
Everyone needs respect.

May 3

After he had dismissed them, he went up on a mountainside by himself to Pray. When evening came, he was there alone.

Matthew 14:23

Father in heaven,
Thank You for this day;
For home, friends, work and play.
Thank You for Your love and care
That is with me everywhere.
May everything I say and do
Be sweet and good, kind and true. Amen

our Father

Thought

Prayer keeps me close to God.

May 4

"Yet a time is coming, and has now come when the true worshipers will worship the Father in spirit and truth, for they are the kind of worshipers the Father seeks."

John 4:23

Because God is a spirit, you cannot see and touch Him as you can your parents. He shows Himself to you in the scriptures. God made the world, gave the Ten Commandments, and sent His son, Jesus, who lived on earth.

By learning about Jesus, you are learning about God.

Thought
The spirit of Jesus lives in me.

May 5

Tell the righteous it will be well with them, for they will enjoy the fruit of their Deeds.

Isaiah 3:10

Righteous people are happy people. Because they know God loves them, they love themselves and others. They love to laugh and have fun. They are glad to give and thankful for all they receive. Even when things go wrong, righteous people trust in God's goodness.

I bask in the warmth of your smile

Thought

The righteous have God's favor.

May 6

"For God so loved the world that he gave his one and only Son, that whoever believes in him shall not perish but have eternal life."
John 3:16

Open my eyes that I may see
All the truth You have for me.
Open my ears that I may hear
The voices of truth You send so clear.
Open my way that I may bring
A life that is pleasing to Christ, my King.
(Clara H. Scott)

No hands
but
mine,
Lord

Thought
God's word is truth.

May 7

Blessed is the man who makes the Lord his trust, who does not look to the proud, to those who turn aside to false gods.

Psalm 40:4

If someone says to you, "I trust you," what does that mean?
It means that person believes you do what is right and say what is truthful. We can always trust God to keep His promises.

I believe in you

Thought

A happy person trusts God completely.

May 8

Commit to the Lord whatever you do, and your plans will succeed.
Proverbs 16:3

Grown-ups like to ask children, "What do you want to be when you grow up?" That is a hard question. Whatever it is you choose to be, ask God for His guidance and blessing. He will help you succeed.

When I grow up, I'll be... myself, but older.

Good decision

Thought

I want to know God's plan for my life.

May 9

Your word, O Lord, is eternal; it stands firm in the heavens.
Psalm 119:89

Look around you. Everything you can see and touch will pass away. Not one thing your eyes can see will last forever, but God's promises are eternal. God says His words last forever. Love also lasts forever and those who believe in Jesus are promised life that never ends.

The love that I have
is the life that I have

Thought

My spirit lives forever.

May 10

Then Peter came to Jesus and asked, "Lord, how many times shall I forgive my brother when he sins against me? Up to seven times?" Jesus answered, "I tell you, not seven times, but up to seventy seven times:"

Matthew 18:21-22

Our heavenly Father freely forgives when we are truly sorry and ask for forgiveness. We show that we are sorry when we try our best not to do the same thing again.

Thought

I am forgiven and willingly forgive others.

May 11

A righteous man cares for the needs of his animal, but the kindest acts of the wicked are cruel.

Proverbs 12:10

Your pet is a creature God has made. You gave the pet its name and as its owner you get to enjoy and take care of your pet's needs. In return, your pet gives you its trust and love.

Thought

I will give my pet loving care every day.

both ends of my Life
say thank-you

May 12

**Be very careful then, how you live - not as unwise but as wise,
making the most of every opportunity because the days are evil.**
Ephesians 5:15

If a friend said to you, "I really like you a lot," but an hour later gave you such
a shove that you fell down and hurt yourself, what would you think?
Would you say, "Oh, I know he likes me anyway," or
would you say, "You don't act like you like me!"
Our acts have to agree with our words.

Thought

I show I am a good friend by my actions.

May 13

The Lord is far from the wicked, but he hears the prayer of the righteous.

Proverbs 15:29

God hears all prayers but the Bible tells us that God pays special attention to the prayers of those who live good lives.

Thought

Lord, help me to live so that my prayers will go straight to You in heaven.

and it wasn't our fault, Lord. We were nowhere near him at the time of the accident

May 14

In everything I did, I showed you that by this kind of hard work we must help the weak, remembering the words the Lord Jesus himself said, "It is more blessed to give than to receive."

Acts 20:35

I apologized to my friend for waiting so long to thank her for a gift she sent.
Her reply was, "I wasn't waiting for thanks.
I just wanted the gift to make you happy." Let's remember that being thanked is not as important as being a loving giver.

Thought

I will give and forget the gift.

I trust in the prickles you gave me.

May 15

He gives strength to the weary and increases the power of the weak.
Isaiah 40:29

Sometimes when learning is a struggle we may become discouraged.
Don't worry about what you can't do.
Do the best you can. Your best is
all you need to give.

Thought

God blesses my best efforts.

The Morning and evening praise
You .

May 16

...yet I will rejoice in the Lord, I will be joyful in
God my Saviour.

Habakkuk 3:18

Will you choose to be happy today,
Or will you fuss and fret as you play?
Will you think of ways to give back,
Or whine about all that you lack?
Be as happy as you choose today,
It's up to you this day in May.

The fact I can't fly doesn't make me a failure.

Thought

I can make this day of May a happy day.

May 17

"Arise, shine, for your light has come, and the glory of the Lord rises upon you."

Isaiah 60:1

How can anyone know whether or not you are a Christian, a follower of Jesus? They will know you are a Christian by your love.

Thought

This little light of mine, I will let it shine loving beams today.

May 18

Whatever you have learned or received or heard from me, or seen in me – put it into Practice. And the God of peace will be with you.

Philippians 4:9

Learn what is right, do what is right and then
you will enjoy God's blessings.

Thought

God is with all who practice right living.

May 19

"Peace I leave with you; my peace I give you; I do not give to you as the world gives. Do not let not your hearts be troubled, nor let it be afraid."

John 14:27

Everyone is afraid of something. What is it that you are afraid of? Jesus tells us over and over again in the Bible, "Do not fear." One time He and His disciples were in a boat when a terrible storm came up. The disciples trembled with fear but Jesus was asleep. They woke Him up saying, "Master, don't you care that we are about to sink?" Jesus answered, "Why are you so frightened and have so little faith?" Then He stood up and caused the waves to grow calm. (Matthew 8:23-26)

Help

Jesus and I are in the same boat

Thought
I will turn my fears over to Jesus
and watch them disappear.

May 20

**The Lord will keep you from all harm - he will watch over your life.
The Lord will watch over your coming and going both now
and for evermore.**

Psalm 121:7

The people who take care of you are special people. Besides parents and grandparents there are baby-sitters whose job it is to be with you and see that you have everything you need.

People who take good care of you
are special blessings.

Wash one
another's
feet

.. including
those with
bunions

Thought

Lord, I'm thankful for all those who give loving care.

May 21

The Lord is good to those whose hope is in him, to the one who seeks him.

Lamentations 3:25

Hide and Seek is a fun game to play. We have to look for them in many places. It is the same when we seek God.

Some of the places to find God are in the Bible, the church, in the beauty of nature, and in quiet times of prayer.

Thought

Lord, I will seek You with my whole heart today. Amen

May 22

...Test everything. Hold on to the good.

1 Thessalonians 5:21

Be careful little eyes what you see,

Be careful little ears what you hear,

Be careful little mouth what you say,

Be careful little hands what you do.

Thought

I will turn away from anything that is evil.

May 23

Therefore encourage one another and build each other up, just as in fact you are doing.
1 Thessalonians 5:11

Nobody likes to be around a faultfinder – a person who always points out what is wrong. It's much more fun to be with someone who points to the good we've done and gives us praise and encouragement.

Thought

Today I will be a person who looks for the good.

May 24

Anyone who listens to the word but does not do what it says is like a man who looks at his face in a mirror and, after looking at himself, goes away and immediately forgets what he looks like.

James 1:23-24

Get a mirror and look at your face. Frown and notice how mean you look.
Smile and notice how much nicer you look.
What kind of face will you show the world today?

I do look good if you tell me so.

Thought

"Smile and the world smiles with you."

May 25

Sing joyfully to the Lord, you righteous; it is fitting for the upright to praise him.

Psalm 33:1

What do people do when they are happy? Why, they sing, of course. What happy song do you like to sing as you go about your work and play?

Thought

I will sing praises to God.

May 26

After he had dismissed them, he went up to a mountainside by himself to pray. When evening came, he was there alone.

Matthew 14:23

When you are alone and have no one to play with, this is a good time to pray, look at a book, listen to some music or just daydream and enjoy your own company.

From here you can see TEN Commandments

Or two, if you look closer

Thought

With Jesus as my unseen friend
I cannot be lonely.

May 27

...he will swallow up death forever; the Sovereign Lord will wipe away the tears from all faces.

Isaiah 25:8

Has anyone ever said to you, "Don't be a crybaby?" What they mean is, don't use crying to get your own way or just to make someone feel sorry for you.

Tears are okay if you're hurting, but nobody wants to be with a crybaby.

Come to me, all who travail, and find Life a burden

I wouldn't go anywhere else

The Lord himself is my helper. Therefore I cannot be afraid

Thought

I will choose to be brave.

May 28

There by the Ahava Canal, I proclaimed a fast, so that we might humble ourselves before our God and to ask him for a safe journey for us and our children, with all our possessions.

Ezra 8:21

Most of the time traveling is fun. Sometimes, though, we think that we will never get to where we are going. We keep asking or thinking, "Are we almost there?" The happiest travelers are those who refuse to complain. They exercise patience and enjoy the journey.

Thought

Lord, give us safe and happy travels. Amen

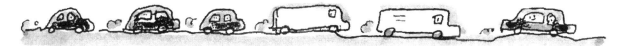

May 29

A wise son heeds his father's instruction, but a mocker does not listen to rebuke.

Proverbs 13:1

As you grow up you are learning things that will become good habits to have all through life.

Can you name some of the good habits you have learned?

Thought

An action often repeated becomes a habit.

May 30

Worship the Lord with gladness; come before him with joyful songs.
Psalm 100:2

For the beauty of the earth;
For the glory of the skies;
For the love which from our birth
Over and around us lies;
Lord of all, to Thee we raise
This our hymn or grateful praise.
(Hymn by F. Pierpoint)

Thought

I will praise God for all blessings.

May 31

May the favor of the Lord our God rest upon us...
Psalm 90:17

We know we have God's favor
when we do our best to live as
Jesus taught us.

"I'm doing my best, Jesus"

Thought

I will do my best for Jesus today.

June 1

"Now learn this lesson from the fig tree: As soon as its twigs get tender and the leaves come out, you know that summer is near."
Matthew 24:32

Summer is here. We no longer need sweaters and caps.
It is vacation time—days to spend outdoors, at the beach,
or just in your own backyard.

God created the changing seasons. Thank Him for
something you especially enjoy about summer.

Thought
Hooray for summer fun!

June 2

Jesus answered, "It is written: 'Man does not live on bread alone, but on every word that comes from the mouth of God.'"
Matthew 4:4

Many holy people wrote the Bible, and God guided each one of them. God wanted us to know Him and His Son, Jesus Christ, and to know how much He loves us.

Thought

The Bible tells of God's love.

June 3

**So be careful to do what the Lord your God has commanded you;
do not turn aside to the right or to the left.**

Deuteronomy 5:32

What are God's laws? They are the Ten Commandments given for
us to hear, learn and obey. The people of Israel heard them first.
Today those of us who hear them will obey them if we are wise.
The Ten Commandments may be found in Exodus 20:1-26.

Thought
The Ten Commandments teach
us right from wrong.

June 4

Surely God is my help; the Lord is the one who sustains me.
Psalm 54:4

"Practice makes perfect," means that even if something seems too hard,you can learn to do it if you will just keep practicing and have God's help.

Thought
I can do great things with
God's help.

June 5

Let us not become weary in doing good, for at the proper time we will reap a harvest if we do not give up.

Galatians 6:9

The patient child said, "I will cheerfully wait my turn." The impatient child said, "Hurry! You are too slow!"

Though it is not always easy to be patient and polite, by waiting cheerfully and listening to others, we will in time become the patient people God would like us to be.

Thought

Love is patient and kind.

June 6

...for every animal of the forest is mine, and the cattle on a thousand hills.

Psalm 50:10

Animals don't understand our words so well as they understand our tone of voice. Loud angry words make our pets run away, but soft-spoken words make them want to be with us. Listen to your voice when you speak. Does it sound soft or does it sound harsh?

Thought

Harsh words stir up fear.

I listen to the sound of your voice ... not just the words

June 7

...in all your ways acknowledge him, and he will make your paths straight.

Proverbs 3:6

The Bible is full of God's promises to us.
We put God first by asking Him to help us in everything we do.

It is God who shows us how to succeed.

Thought
God waits for me to ask His help.

June 8

The Lord detests lying lips, but he delights in men who are truthful.
Proverbs 12:22

A promise to someone is something to take seriously. Just as God keeps His promises to us, we must also be sure to keep our promises.

Thought
I will be a promise keeper.

June 9

You guide me with your counsel, and afterward you will take me into glory.

Psalm 73:24

At times when you can't decide what you should do, ask yourself this – 'What would Jesus do?' He is our best example.

Thought

I will try to be like Jesus.

June 10

The Lord has rewarded me according to my righteousness, according to the cleanness of my hands in his sight.

Psalm 18:24

What is better, a clean room or a messy one?

Which kind of room do you suppose is more pleasing to God?

God made His world in perfect order and beautiful.

You can clean up your room without being asked and enjoy order and neatness.

Thought

I will do my best to be neat.

June 11

**For a thousand years in your sight are like a day that has just gone by,
or like a watch in the night.**

Psalm 90:4

Yesterday is gone. We are unable to change anything that happened.
Tomorrow is unknown. We cannot be absolutely sure what will happen tomorrow.

Today is the precious time that is truly ours.
Live this day so that when tomorrow comes you
will remember the good times and be glad.

Thought

I'm thankful for today.

June 12

The Lord is near to all who call on him, to all who call on him in truth.
Psalm 145:18

Don't let this day go by without a word to your heavenly Father.
Your word may be, "thanks" or "help" or "protect".
God is waiting to hear from you.
Ask or say whatever you will.
God delights to hear the prayers of
His children.

but I LIKE you
to trouble
me.

Thought

God wants to hear my prayer.

June 13

He who has ears, let him hear.

Matthew 11:15

Everyone likes to hear good news. In the Bible the good news books are Matthew, Mark, Luke and John. The good news is about Jesus Christ – His birth, His death, and His rising from the dead.

The best news is that because He lives, we will live forever, too.

Thought

The Bible is a book of good news.

Because I live, you shall live also.

June 14

I have fought the good fight, I have finished the race,
I have kept the faith;

2 Timothy 4:7

I will only worry about pleasing you.

After Jesus went to heaven his apostles decided to write down the important things He taught. It is called the Apostles Creed. The creed begins, "I believe in God, the Father Almighty, maker of heaven and earth and in Jesus Christ, His only Son, our Lord."

Thought
I believe in God and I trust in Jesus Christ.

June 15

A gentle answer turns away wrath, but a harsh word stirs up anger.

Proverbs 15:1

If someone says, "I hate you",
how do you feel inside?
Of course you feel hurt or angry.
Words have power. They have power
to hurt us or to help us.

Thought

I will speak words today that help others.

Preach the gospel
to every creature

use words if
necessary.

June 16

**Therefore confess your sins to each other and pray for each other
so that you may be healed.
The prayer of a righteous man is powerful and effective.**

James 5:16

Do you know someone who is sick, discouraged or
suffering in any way?

Your secret sincere prayer for that person can
bring God's help and blessing.

KINDEST

VERY KIND

KIND

I want to be THIS tall."

Thought
"Lord, help me live from day to day,
In such a self-forgetful way
That even when I kneel to pray,
My prayer shall be for others."
Charles D. Meigs

June 17

The way of a fool seems right to him, but a wise man listens to advice.
Proverbs 12:15

The pussycat missed seeing what she went to London to see because
she kept playing with a silly mouse. When you are on vacation,
don't be like the pussycat that missed all the best.
Enjoy the new sights, the new sounds and the new tastes.

I imagine you've come
to see me.

Pussycat, pussycat, where have you been?
I've been to London to look at the queen.
Pussycat, pussycat, what did you there?
I frightened a little mouse under her chair.

Thought
I will make the most of every opportunity.

June 18

Do not lie to each other, since you have taken off the old self with its practices and have put on the new self, which is being renewed in knowledge in the image of its Creator.

Colossians 3:9-10

God never tempts you to tell a lie.

The tempter is the devil himself.

The devil is delighted when we decide to be dishonest.

When the devil tempts you to lie, just say,

"No, I choose to be truthful."

'Now give me sense to heed your laws.. sense your laws...

Thought

I will say "No" when tempted.

June 19

So encourage one another and build each other up, just as in fact you are doing.

1 Thessalonians 5:11

"My doll is prettier than yours!" or, "I have more trucks than you." This is bragging and an unkind way to behave.

Be quick to say nice things about others rather than about yourself.

Thought

I will not brag.

June 20

...let the wise listen and add to their learning, and let the discerning get guidance.

Proverbs 1:5

How high can you count? And do you know your ABC's?
Think how proud you are to have learned so much.
The wise child will always find fun in learning.

Thought

I will learn something new today.

I am taking a degree
in higher mathematics.

June 21

And we know that in all things God works for the good of those who love him, who have been called according to his purpose.
Romans 8:28

Next time you put together a puzzle pretend that each piece is a part of your life. For a while you don't know how it all fits together, but God knows.

He promises to fit all the pieces together perfectly if we love and serve Him. (Romans 8:28)

Thought

I serve and trust God with my life.

June 22

I will instruct you and teach you in the way you should go;
I will counsel you and watch over you.

Psalm 32:8

Have you heard of the game,
"Follow the Leader"?
Whatever the leader does the followers
try to do it too. We have a Leader whose
name is Jesus. He is the perfect example.

DON'T GO WITHOUT ME, JESUS.

Thought

I have decided to follow Jesus.

June 23

It is good to praise the Lord, and make music to your name; O most high, to proclaim your love in the morning, and your faithfulness at night.

Psalm 92:1-2

Add to your good habits a prayer of praise each morning for
God's greatness, and in the evening a prayer of thanks for
His goodness to you during the day.

Thought

I have much to be thankful for.

Arise, shine, for your light has come

June 24

"My dear children, I write this to you so that you will not sin. But if anybody does sin, we have one who speaks to the Father in our defense -- Jesus Christ, the Righteous One.

1 John 2:1

When you and I deliberately choose to do wrong, we not only hurt ourselves but we end up hurting other people. The person who steals, the drunk driver who causes an accident, the neighbor who gossips, all hurt others as well as themselves.

Some people push you off the world, others help you to get on.

Thought
My behavior and words affect others.

June 25

On my bed I remember you; I think of you through the watches of the night.

Psalm 63:6

Think how many things in the world are completely silent—the sun, moon, stars, trees, plants, rocks, hills and the deepest feelings within our hearts.

Thought

I will make time for silence.

Whatever part of the sky you're in, you can always shine.

June 26

Great is the Lord, and most worthy of praise, in the city of our God, his holy mountain.

Psalm 48:1

God has many names.
Some of His names are Creator, Father, King, Lord, Judge, Light, Defender, the Word and the Holy Spirit.

Many Names, one Redeemer

Thought

God is great and God is good.

June 27

For it is not those who hear the law who are righteous in God's sight, but it is those who obey the law who will be declared righteous.

Romans 2:13

Reading the Bible, going to church, praying, even doing good works does not prove that you are righteous in God's sight. How then can one tell whether a person is a true follower of Christ? Jesus answered that question by saying "All men will know you are my disciples if you love one another." (John 13:35)

Thought

When I act with love I please my heavenly Father.

June 28

The Jesus told his disciples a parable to show them that they should always pray and not give up.

Luke 18:1

Remember how good you felt when you finally learned how to swim without a life preserver? You wanted to tell everyone, "I did it! I did it!" Being able to swim was worth all your effort.

Thought

If at first you don't succeed, try, try again!

she's done it

June 29

Be devoted to one another in brotherly love. Honor one another above yourselves."

Romans 12:10

Jesus has the Last Word

Love

Jesus taught us over and over that we are to love others. You show your love when you are kind, helpful and unselfish.

Thought

I will live in a loving way today.

June 30

**And do not set your heart on what you will eat or drink;
do not worry about it.**

Luke 12:29

Giver of all crumbs
and tit-bits, I sing your
praise.

Our heavenly Father cares about the
little things in our lives as well as the
big things. We can talk to Him about
anything that is on our minds.

What is on your mind today?
Whatever it is, God cares about that too.

Thought

I can talk to God about anything.

July 1

"Why were you searching for me?" he asked. "Didn't you know I had to be in my Father's house?"

Luke 2:49

From the time God created Adam until now only one person lived a perfect life. That person is Jesus.

He knew from the time He was young that He was born to do the will of His heavenly Father.

Thought
God has a plan for my life.

July 2

He who is kind to the poor man lends to the Lord, and he will reward him for what he has done.

Proverbs 19:17

Preach the gospel to every creature — use words if necessary.

Many in the world do not have enough to eat or a place to live. We who have homes and plenty to eat can help those who are needy.

Thought
I will show kindness to the needy.

July 3

Do your best to present yourself to God as one approved, a workman who does not need to be ashamed and who correctly handles the word of truth.
2 Timothy 2:15

Do you like to help with the daily chores such as picking up toys or putting away the dishes?

Your willingness to do your part shows your love and caring for your family.

Thought
I will do each chore the best I know how.

July 4

Shout for joy to the Lord, all the earth. Worship the Lord with gladness; come before him with joyful songs.

Psalm 100:1-2

The 4th of July—a great day to fly the American flag or watch a parade. Today is our country's birthday. A good prayer or hymn to sing is "God bless America, land that I love, Stand beside her and guide her, Through the night with a light from above."

Thought
Today I will celebrate my country's birthday.

July 5

**For he will command his angels concerning you to guard you
in all your ways.**
Psalm 91:11

Have you ever seen an angel? Angels live in heaven but there
are also angels without wings who live among us.

When we say, "Oh, you're an angel,"
we're saying that person is full of goodness.
Do you know someone who reminds you of an angel?

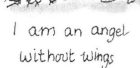

I am an angel
without wings

Thought
I can be an angel to someone today.

July 6

Great is the Lord, and most worthy of praise, in the city of our God, his holy mountain.

Psalm 48:1

All things bright and beautiful,
All creatures great and small,
All things wise and wonderful,
The Lord God made them all.
Each little flower that opens,
Each little bird that sings,
He made their glowing colors;
He made their tiny wings.
He gave us eyes to see them
And lips that we might tell
How great is God Almighty
Who has made all things well.
Cecil Alexander

Thought
Our world is a beautiful place.

July 7

But a Samaritan, as he traveled, came where the man was; and when he saw him, he took pity on him. He went to him and bandaged his wounds, pouring on oil and wine. Then he put the man on his own donkey and took him to an inn and took care of him.

Luke 10:33-34

Jesus told his disciples the story of the good Samaritan. Lots of so-called good people passed by the poor man who had been robbed and beaten. But not the good Samaritan! He stopped, took care of his wounds, and then took the man to a place where he would be safe. The Samaritan got him medicine for his wounds, and left some money for his care.

We don't know the words of the good Samaritan, but we do know that he showed kindness by the help he gave.

It's not my fault, Lord. I didn't knock him down.

Thought

It's not what I say that counts; it's what I do.

July 8

And God said, "Let the water teem with living creatures, and let birds fly above the earth across the expanse of the sky."
Genesis 1:20

All the creatures God made add so much beauty and wonder to our world. One way to show our love for God is to treat animals with care and love.

Thought
I'll think of something nice to do for my pet today.

July 9

...there is a friend who sticks closer than a brother.

Proverbs 18:24

Make all the friends you can,

Keep all the friends you make,

And when you meet a stranger,

Give his hand a hearty shake.

For all the countless treasures

Which in time may come your way,

There'll be nothing quite as precious

As the friends you make today.

Thought

A friend is a special blessing.

July 10

**"It is good to praise the Lord and make music to your name,
O Most High.**

Psalm 92:1

When you think about the blessings you receive each
day at home, at school and at play, remember God is
the source of all good.

Thought

My blessings are many.

Christianity is the best
policy.

July 11

"See that you do not look down on one of these little ones. For I tell you that their angels in heaven always see the face of my Father in heaven."
Matthew 18:10

Jesus always had time for children
and gave them his blessing.

Children are special citizens in God's kingdom. (Matthew 18:4)

Thought
Jesus loves me this I know, for the Bible tells me so.

July 12

"But you, Bethlehem, land of Judah, are by no means least among the rulers of Judah; for out of you will come forth a ruler who will shepherd my people Israel."

Matthew 2:6

Do you know the name of the leader of your country?

Our leaders need our prayers that they may lead our country well.

Thought

I will pray for our leaders today.

July 13

You will have plenty to eat, until you are full, and you will praise the name of the Lord your God, who has worked wonders for you; never again will my people be shamed.

Joel 2:26

Some favorite summer treats we all enjoy are a slice of cold red watermelon, a frosty ice cream cone, fresh picked blackberries, strawberries and cream, and the taste of a juicy peach.

What special summer treats do you enjoy?

Thought

I love the taste of summer fruits.

July 14

All spoke well of him and were amazed at the gracious words that came from his lips. "Isn't this Joseph's son?" they asked.

Luke 4:22

Jesus worked with His father, Joseph, in their carpenter's shop and worshipped with His family in the synagogue. He knew the scriptures well.

Even when He was very young, He knew that He wanted to do His heavenly Father's work.

Thought

I, too, can grow up in God's favor.

No strength but YOURS'

July 15

**On that day you will realize that I am in my Father,
and you are in me, and I am in you.**

John 14:20

Has anyone ever said to you, "Why you look just like your Mom or Dad?"
The truth is you look just the way God made you. You did not choose to be
short or tall, have brown eyes or blue. God created you to be special and
unique—one of a kind. God also created you in His image. As you follow
Jesus day by day others will begin to recognize Christ's character in you.

Thought

I am growing in wisdom
and in stature.

July 16

A happy heart makes the face cheerful, but heartache crushes the spirit.
Proverbs 15:13

A smile is a gift you can give to another person anytime.
The gift costs nothing but can do wonders.
Jean Lovett said, "A smile is a curve that can
straighten out a lot of things."

Thought
When I see someone without a smile,
I will give one of mine.

July 17

Let the wise listen and add to their learning.
Proverbs 1:5

It's good to ask questions because that's how we learn.
The world is full of books, and now the Internet that contains
all kinds of knowledge.

There is only One who has all the answers,
though, and that One is God.

Thought
All knowledge comes from God.

July 18

Let us not become weary in doing good, for at the proper time we will reap a harvest if we do not give up.

Galatians 6:9

Summer travel is fun. Besides a suitcase full of clothes each of us can take along some things that do not have to be packed which will make our trip a good one. On your trip take along patience when you think you'll never get where you're going. Take along cheerfulness when you're served peas and you'd rather have corn. Take along a helpful attitude when you see another person struggling.

Taking all I need for the journey.

Thought

I will be a joyful traveler.

July 19

If we confess our sins, he is faithful and just and will forgive us our sins and purify us from all unrighteousness.

1 John 1:9

"Don't blame me! I didn't do it, she did it!"
In other words, "I refuse to admit that I did anything wrong."
A grade school teacher scolded her student for not doing the
assigned homework. The student's excuse was,
"The television was playing too loud." The teacher said,
"You must not blame your failure on someone else."
It's a lesson worth remembering.

Thought
I will not blame others.

July 20

When I was a child, I talked like a child, I thought like a child,
I reasoned like a child.
When I became a man, I put childish ways behind me.

1 Corinthians 13:11

Listen to younger children. They often yell, "Mine!", when they are playing.
Sharing is something they haven't learned. As they grow older,
little children learn more about sharing.

Thought
The older I am,
the wiser I become.

July 21

"Peace, peace to those far and near." says the Lord. "And I will heal them."
Isaiah 57:19

Some people choose to go through life quarreling and fighting.
They have not learned to live happily with others.
There can be no real peace on earth until
everyone learns to treat others fairly.

Thought

Let peace on earth begin with me today.

July 22

...for they loved the praise from men more than praise from God.
John 12:43

Each of us has a need to feel approved by others. Our parents' approval keeps us obeying and doing the right thing. Our friends' approval too, makes us feel good about ourselves. The scriptures teach that the approval of God is more important than the approval of any other human. We know we have God's approval when we obey His commands and love Him with all our hearts.

Who can stand against such faith?

I believe in you

And I believe in you.

Thought
I will strive to
please God above all.

July 23

Guard the good deposit that was entrusted to you – guard it with the help of the Holy Spirit who lives in us.

2 Timothy 1:14

Do you ever look at someone a few years older than you and feel unhappy with yourself just because you are younger? The older person is allowed to stay up later or go places that you wish you could go.

You may not realize it, but for right now you are perfect just the way you are.

Thought
I am perfect in
God's eyes.

July 24

But encourage one another daily, as long as it is called Today, so that none of you may be hardened by sin's deceitfulness.

Hebrews 3:13

The apostle Paul did not always encourage Christians. There was a time when he hated Christians, and even tried to kill them. One day as he was traveling to Damascus, Paul heard God's voice telling him to become His messenger. From that time Paul changed.
He no longer hated Christians but began to follow Christ.
He became the writer of most of the New Testament.
All of His writings are words of encouragement to Christians.

Where am I?
Who are you?

A funny thing happened to me on the way to Damascus

DAMASCUS
XII n

Thought
I will speak a word of encouragement today.

July 25

Avoid every kind of evil.

1 Thessalonians 5:22

As a child I helped in my Daddy's store. He gave me permission to take money from the cash register when I needed it. My friend noticed my taking money out when I needed it for the movies or the skating rink. She believed I must have been stealing. One day some money was missing at her house. She asked me if I had taken it and explained why she believed I might have done so. Of course, I was surprised and hurt to be accused of stealing, but I learned a valuable lesson.

I learned that our actions could easily appear evil or wrong to others.

Thought

I will avoid anything that appears evil.

July 26

Jesus answered, "I am the way, and the truth and the life.

No one comes to the Father except through Me."

John 14:6

Tell me the stories of Jesus
I love to hear.
Things I would ask Him to tell me
If He were here;
Scenes by the wayside, tales of the sea
Stories of Jesus, tell them to me.

First let me hear how the children
Stood 'round His knee,
And I shall fancy His blessing
Resting on me;
Words full of kindness, deeds full of grace,
All in the love light of Jesus face.

(Frederic A. Challinor)

Thought

I like learning about Jesus.

July 27

And the boy Samuel continued to grow in stature and in favor with the Lord and with men.

1 Samuel 2:26

Once upon a time there was a wise little boy named Samuel.
In his quiet times he spoke to God and said,
"Speak Lord, I am listening."

Too often I say, "Listen Lord,
I am speaking."

Thought
Today I will practice being a good listener.

July 28

Jesus Christ is the same yesterday and today and forever.
Hebrews 13:8

Yesterday is gone forever. Tomorrow is uncertain. Today is a gift.
Is that why it's called "the present"?

Thought
I will enjoy this gift of today.

YOU DON'T REALLY NEED
TO SPELL ANYTHING ELSE.

July 29

**The earth is the Lord's, and everything in it, the world,
and all who live in it.**

Psalm 24:1

Oh, give me a home where the buffalo roam;
Where the deer and the antelope play.
Where seldom is heard a discouraging word
And the skies are not cloudy all day.

Thought
I will do my best to keep our world beautiful.

July 30

Honor your father and your mother, so that you may live long in the land which the Lord your God is giving you.

Exodus 20:12

But this is your house too, daddy.

God commands children to honor their fathers and mothers. We honor them by speaking to them with respect, never being sassy or rude. We honor them by our obedience and by growing in love.

Thought

I honor my parents just as they honor Jesus.

July 31

I am the vine, you are the branches. If a man remains in me, and I in him, he will bear much fruit; apart from me you can do nothing.

John 15:5

The minute you pick a piece of fruit off the tree or the vine; that fruit no longer grows. For a piece of fruit to get to its best taste and flavor it must remain attached to the tree or vine.

Thought

When I stay close to Jesus I grow in love, joy, peace, patience, kindness, goodness and self-control.

August 1

"...But as for me and my household, we will serve the Lord."
Joshua 24:15

Choices, Choices! Have you ever had difficulty choosing and said to yourself, "There are just too many choices?" Each day you choose what you think about, what you will say, and how you will act. God can help you make wise choices when you ask His help.

Thought
I will ask Jesus, "What would You do, Lord?".

Was there anything you particularily wanted to say?

August 2

A gentle answer turns away wrath, but a harsh word stirs up anger.

Proverbs 15:1

What do you do when someone yells at you? Are you tempted to shout back?
The Bible teaches us that it's better to give a soft answer.

Thought

I will not answer in anger.

August 3

Do you not know that your body is a temple of the Holy Spirit, who is in you, whom you have received from God? You are not your own; you were bought at a price. Therefore honor God with your body.

1 Corinthians 6:19

It is important for our good health to eat many different foods,
not just the same thing everyday.
God made an almost endless variety
of fruits, vegetables,
and grains for us to enjoy.

Thought

I will try a new food today that God has created.

August 4

(Jesus said) "Give, and it will be given to you. A good measure, pressed down, shaken together and running over, will be poured into your lap. For with the measure you use, it will be measured to you."

Luke 6:38

God's blessings are new every morning. He blesses each of us with life, health, food, clothing, homes, family, friends, and laughter. Just as God has freely blessed us, we are expected to be generous in our giving of ourselves to others.

Thought

To love is to give.

August 5

And so we know and rely on the love God has for us. God is love. Whoever lives in love lives in God and God in him.

1 John 4:16

"I have to live with myself, and so I want to be fit for myself to know," the poem begins. You are God's own child and because He loves you, you know that you are lovable.

Thought

I am a loving member of God's family.

August 6

For these commands are a lamp, this teaching is a light, and the corrections of discipline are the way to life.

Proverbs 6:23

King Solomon, the wisest of men in his day, said that God's commands are like the flash-light (or lamp). Without His commands we grope around living dark sin-filled lives. When we learn to obey God's laws, we no longer walk in darkness but live in the light of God's presence.

Thought

God's laws light my way.

August 7

**"Have I not commanded you? Be strong and courageous.
Do not be terrified; do not be discouraged, for the Lord your God will
be with you wherever you go."**

Joshua 1:9

I'm coming as well as I
can, Jesus

After Moses died Joshua became the leader of God's
people, the Israelites. God saw Joshua's faith, courage,
obedience, and devotion to God's laws. God also saw
that Joshua had fear and doubt! The enemies all around
him were strong and Moses who had walked so closely
with God had died. God gave Joshua a pep talk.
He commanded him to be strong, not to tremble
and not to be dismayed.

Thought

Joshua succeeded when God led the way.

August 8

**There is a time for everything, and a season for
every activity under heaven:**
Ecclesiastes 3:1

In Ecclesiastes Chapter 3 it talks about the fact that there is a right time for everything. There is a right time to sleep, a right time to awaken, a time to work, a time to rest, a time to listen, a time to talk, a time to pray and a time to praise, a time to visit and a time to be alone.

Please feel free to pop in for a chat

I never said I'd come first

Thought
There is a time and place
for everything.

August 9

A false witness will not go unpunished, and he who pours out lies will not go free.

Proverbs 19:9

Why tell the truth? God commands us to be truthful,
and others expect us to tell the truth.
Telling lies is a big mistake. It always gets us into trouble.
Be the person others can trust and believe. A truthful person pleases God
and does not disappoint others.

Thought
I will be truthful because
others trust me.

August 10

Your word is a lamp to my feet and a lamp for my path.
Psalm 119:105

Before your parents set out on a long trip in their automobile, they get out their map and decide which highways they will travel. The map keeps them going in the right direction and gets them where they are going in the shortest time. God has given us a road map for living our daily lives. He knows all the paths that are unfamiliar to us; He can turn our darkness into light, protect us from danger, and see that we arrive happily. God's map book for our lives is in the Bible.

Thought
God will lead me on right paths.

August 11

For where you have envy and selfish ambition, there you find disorder and every evil practice.

James 3:16

Your brother or sister gets more attention than you get from your parents. Or your friend's bike is newer and nicer than your own. Or your friend's Mom is always home, but your Mom must work. You feel jealous and unhappy, envious and begin to feel sorry for yourself. When you dwell on these selfish feelings, the door is open for evil to enter your spirit. Refuse jealous feelings. Ask God to help you replace them with love. Pray for those you envy.

Refuse to allow jealousy to destroy your goodness.

Thought

Jealousy opens the door to evil.

August 12

You will go out in joy and be led forth in peace;
the mountains and hills will burst into song before you,
and all the trees of the field will clap their hands.

Isaiah 55:12

Does the scripture you have just heard remind you of the joy of summer?
The outdoors is warm and beautiful, birds chirp, butterflies wave in passing,
and trees are heavy with great tasting fruit.

God delights in the joy and fun that
August brings you and me.

Thought
I love the days of summer.

August 13

Though you have not seen him, you love him; and even though you do not see him now, but believe in him, and are filled with an inexpressible and glorious joy.

1 Peter 1:8

Have you ever heard a person say, "I'd have to see that to believe it?" It's easy to believe something we can see with our own eyes. After Jesus died on the cross he rose from the dead and appeared to ten of his disciples. They could see him yet they thought they were looking at a ghost. He had to prove He was alive by telling them to touch His scarred hands, feet and side. He then asked for food and ate with them. (Luke 24:38-43)

When they told Thomas all that had happened he still could not believe that Jesus could be alive again. Thomas doubted until he touched Jesus with his own hands.

Thought
I do not have to see to believe.

I do not have
to see

Touching is
believing

August 14

The wicked man flees though no one is pursuing, but the righteous are as bold as a lion.

Proverbs 28:1

Has anyone ever said to you, "Don't be a fraidy-cat!"
The Bible teaches us a lot about fear. We who are God's children are to be as bold as a lion.

How can we be "fraidy-cats" when God is our leader?

I like playing follow my leader

Thought
There's a lot of difference between a "fraidy-cat" and a lion.

August 15

Be happy, young man, while you are young, and let your heart give you joy in the days of your youth.

Ecclesiastes 11:9

Live, laugh and be happy every day. Enjoy the carefree days of your childhood. When you make good choices and turn away from wrong or evil you are paving the way for a good life. God will eventually punish those who give no thought to obeying His laws.

Thought
My future success depends on my good choices and God's blessings.

August 16

Forgive as the Lord forgave you.

Colossians 3:13

It's easy to love those who love us, take care of us, play with us, and do nice things for us. It's harder to love those who aren't friendly, who treat us unkindly and are downright mean.

We need God's help to love as He teaches us to do.

Thought

I want to be loving and forgiving.

Jesus wants me to forgive you
seventy times seven

August 17

And this is what he promised us—even eternal life.

1 John 2:25

Our bodies need food, water, exercise and rest to be
healthy, but our bodies are not intended to last forever.
Our loving spirit that trusts and believes Jesus' words will
never die but live forever and ever.

An Apple
a day keeps
the doctor
away

GOOD
Deeds

Thought
I will take care of my body, mind, and
especially my loving spirit, because my
spirit lives forever.

August 18

For he chose us in him before the creation of the world to be holy and blameless in his sight.

Ephesians 1:4

Wow! God made you and me holy just as He is holy.
We may fail at times to always do the right thing, but
we know God loves and forgives us.
God accepts us as His holy children.

Thought
Nothing can separate me from
Christ's love.

August 19

...for they loved praise from men more than praise from God.
John 12:43

The people loved Jesus. They wanted to make Him an earthly king.
They shouted "Hosanna!" –a word meaning praise and honor as
he entered Jerusalem. But Jesus did not love their praise more
than he loved God's approval.
Above all, Jesus lived to please God,
even if it meant His physical death.

Thought

The approval of God lasts forever and ever.

August 20

Remember the Sabbath day by keeping it holy.

Exodus 20:8

Six days of the week it is God's plan for us to work. After our six days

of work we are to enjoy a day of rest. This is the day

for going to church, worship and recreation.

Thought

I was glad when they said unto me,

"Let us go into the house of the Lord."

to do my best I need some rest

SUNDAY
MONDAY   TUESDAY   WEDNESD
FRIDAY   THURS
SATUR

August 21

As long as the earth endures, seedtime and harvest, cold and heat, summer and winter, day and night will never cease."

Genesis 8:22

Have you noticed that all fruits and
vegetables have seeds?
We do the planting of the seeds and
God makes them grow and bear fruit.

Thought

Every garden is God's miracle.

August 22

...but God disciplines us for our good, that we may share in his holiness.

Hebrews 12:10

I would follow you Jesus, but I'm rather tied up at present

Our Father in heaven hates wrong actions that are hurtful. The Bible teaches that our wrong actions will be corrected.

Just as a loving parent corrects our wrong behavior, so does God teaches us and correct His children.

Thought
When I am corrected I will remember it is
to teach me right from wrong.

August 23

"...for God so loved the world that he gave his one and only Son that whoever believes in him shall not perish but have eternal life."

John 3:1-16

You will remember Bible verses that you learn now even when you are many years older. Have you memorized the Ten Commandments and John 3:16?

It's a good way to keep God's truth in your heart.

Thought
I will not forget
God's teachings.

August 24

A fool shows his annoyance at once, but a prudent man overlooks an insult.

Proverbs 12:16

How do you act when the person you are playing with refuses to share or take turns? Do you make a big fuss and run to tell your parent or the teacher? A better way may be to say, "Excuse me, but I've been waiting a long time for my turn." You will be happier if you don't insist on your own way even when you are right.

"EXCUSE ME. but I've been waiting six weeks."

Well, it seems like six

Thought
I am willing to overlook others' bad manners.

August 25

But our citizenship is in heaven. And we eagerly await a Savior from there, the Lord Jesus Christ.

Philippians 3:20

Don't you just love to visiting cousins you haven't seen in a long time? When you spend time with your favorite people you feel glad and happy.

This is how you will feel when you get to heaven where Jesus lives.

Thought
In Heaven there will be no more tears, sickness or goodbyes.

August 26

The good man brings good things out of the good stored up in his heart. For out of the overflow of his heart his mouth speaks.

Luke 6:45

Those who pretend to be good may fool others for a short time, but sooner or later their own words will prove whether they are good or evil.

Thought

If my heart is right, my words will prove it.

August 27

Jesus knowing their thoughts, took a little child and had him stand beside him. Then he said to them, "Whoever welcomes this little child in my name welcomes me; and whoever welcomes me welcomes the one who sent me. For he who is least among you all—he is the greatest."

Luke 9:47-48

Those who give loving care to children
are great in God's eyes.

"I'll have some of that, please."

Thought
Jesus loves all the
children of the world.

August 28

"So I say to you: Ask and it will be given to you; seek and you will find; knock and the door will be opened to you."

Luke 11:9

The person who keeps on asking God, praying for His help, and depending on him will receive God's blessings.

Thought
God helps those who keep on calling Him for help.

August 29

Then he said to them, "Watch out! Be on your guard against all kinds of greed; a man's life does not consist in the abundance of his possessions."

Luke 12:15

Sometimes there seems to be no end to our "want list".
We want what we see on TV, think we must have what a friend has,
or what we see in a store. Jesus teaches that getting more things
won't keep us happy for very long.

Thought
I can decide to be happy and thankful for what
I have now rather than always begging for
something new.

August 30

Dear friends, since God so loved us, we also ought to love one another.

1 John 4:11

You are wise if you refuse to compare yourself with others.
Didn't God make each of us different?
Love yourself just the way God made you
and love others the same.

Thought
We're all children of the same
heavenly Father and it is He that
made us perfect in His eyes.

August 31

We know that God does not listen to sinners. He listens to the godly man who does his will.

John 9:31

The person who prays best is the person who truly loves and serves God.

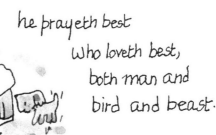

he prayeth best
Who loveth best,
both man and
bird and beast.

Tinkle, TINKLE,

That's what I like to hear

Thought
God hears the prayers of his children who behave lovingly.

September 1

But be very careful to keep the commandment and the law that Moses the servant of the Lord gave you: to love the Lord your God, to walk in all his ways, to obey his commands, to hold fast to him and to serve him with all your heart and all your soul.

Joshua 22:5

How can we show God we love Him?
By obeying His teachings, praying and worshiping
Him and by showing loving kindness to others.

EXCUSE ME,
But I think
there is another
way.

Thought
Living God's way is the best way.

September 2

Do not judge, or you too will be judged.

Matthew 7:1

Only God knows the heart of another person.
Your work is to love and not be quick to criticize.

Thought
I will leave judging
to God.

September 3

A cheerful heart is good medicine, …

Proverbs 17:22

We can help a sick person feel better by saying,
"I hope you will feel better soon. I am praying for you."
Or you might ask, "What can I do for you that
would help? Our cheerful words may be just
the right medicine.

HOW ARE YOU GETTING
ON THESE DAYS ?

Thought

A cheerful word is good medicine.

September 4

He said to me: "It is done. I am the Alpha and the Omega, the Beginning and the End."

Revelations 21:6

One day ends, then another begins. The old year ends and then Another begins and so on. In God there is no beginning or ending. He was before time, is now, and always will be.

In the morning

and in the evening too.

Thought
Every day is a new beginning.

September 5

Indeed, the very hairs of your head are all numbered.
Don't be afraid; you are worth more than many sparrows

Luke 12:7

God has much to say in the Bible about the value of each one of us.
Why God knows even the number of hairs on our heads!
He is interested in every little thing about you and me.

Thought
The world says, "Count everyone".
God says, "Everyone counts".

September 6

Do your best to present yourself to God as one approved, a workman who does not need to be ashamed and who correctly handles the word of truth

2 Timothy 2:15

God approves of me when I'm doing my best and
when I always tell the truth.
Telling the truth is very important.

Thought

I will do my best for God today.

September 7

"A student is not above his teacher, nor a servant above his master."
Matthew 10:24

Your teacher has high hopes for you.
He or she has studied many long years to prepare how best to teach
you the many important things you need to know.

Good teachers deserve respectful
attention, honor, and their
students' best efforts.

Thought
I will pay close attention to everything my teacher says today.

September 8

Whatever you do, work at it with all your heart, as working for the Lord, not for men.

Colossians 3:23

Can work ever be as much fun as play?
Yes, it can when you are happy to
do your best.

as best I know how

Thought

Working will be fun when I do the best job that I can.

September 9

But godliness with contentment is great gain.

1 Timothy 6:6

There's a catchy little tune with the words:
"Oh, we ain't got a barrel of money,
Maybe we're ragged and funny,
But we travel along singing a song side by side.
We don't know what's coming tomorrow,
Maybe it's trouble and sorrow,
But we'll travel along singing a song, side by side."

Sounds as though these travelers are ragged but rich according
to the Bible.
They are singing as they go along their way, willing to share
with their fellow travelers.

Thought

I have riches that money cannot buy.

September 10

...serve one another in love.

Galatians 5:13

Lord, let me live from day to day
In such a self-forgetful way
That even when I kneel to pray
My prayer shall be for others.

Help me in all the work I do
To ever be sincere and true
And know that all the work I do
Must needs be done for others.

Others, Lord yes others,
Let this my motto be.
Help me to live for others that I may be like thee.

–Anonymous

I am among you

as one that serves

Thought

My life can make a difference.

September 11

Whoever can be trusted with very little can also be trusted with much, and whoever is dishonest with very little will also be dishonest with much.

Luke 16:10

Tell "a little white lie," and you're sure to tell a bigger one sometime. In God's eyes there are no little sins.

Thought

I must always say and do what is right.

September 12

...for I know that through your prayers and the help given by the Spirit of Jesus Christ, what has happened to be will turn out for my deliverance.

Philippians 1:19

Do you have a favorite book of fairytales – stories of little elves and fairies with magic powers? These tales stretch our imagination and take us into a world of make-believe.

Hans Christian Anderson, famous fairy tale writer, said, "Everyone's life is a fairytale written by God's finger."

Thought
Life is a delightful adventure

September 13

Dear friend, do not imitate what is evil but what is good. Anyone who does what is good is from God. Anyone who does what is evil has not seen God.

3 John 1:11

Heroes. We all look up to someone. Is your hero a parent, a teacher, a football star or maybe your big brother or sister? Choose your hero wisely. Make sure your hero is a follower of Jesus Christ, the perfect example.

True wisdom lies in knowing which way to go ...

Thought

Jesus Christ is our best example.

September 14

Be strong and take heart, all you who hope in the Lord.

Psalm 31:24

Just how important is hope anyway?

Hope gives you strength and helps you keep going when things are difficult.

Without hope we grope

We always hope and pray and
trust that God will help us.

Thought

When things are difficult I will ask God for help.

September 15

And the boy Samuel continued to grow in stature and in favor with the Lord and with men.

1 Samuel 2:26

Samuel lived in the temple with Eli as his mother had promised. He grew up with Eli's sons who were greedy and disobedient. Eli did not correct and discipline his sons. Samuel saw their disobedience but he was wise enough not to follow in their ways.

Thought
When others misbehave
I won't be a follower.

September 16

Pride goes before destruction, and a haughty spirit before a fall.
Proverbs 16:18

The person who is haughty or "stuck-up" thinks and acts as though he or she is better than others. This is an attitude that displeases God. Jesus never looked down on others but was eager to give a helping hand.

Thought
I will be a friendly person to all.

September 17

Set your minds on things above, not on earthly things.
Colossians 3:2

Each of us struggles to be unselfish rather than selfish, patient rather than impatient, cheerful rather than unhappy and humble rather than proud.

The important thing is that we try hard to be Christlike everyday.

Thought
I like the new me I am becoming.

September 18

For if you forgive men when they sin against you, your heavenly Father will also forgive you.

Matthew 6:14

The Bible teaches is that if we want God to forgive us, we must first forgive others who have wronged us. We all need God's forgiveness, and God will help us be forgiving to others when we ask Him.

But what happens AFTER I've forgiven him seventy times seven ?

Thought
Jesus was quick to forgive others.

September 19

...serve one another with love.

Galatians 5:13

When you see someone who needs help be quick to say, "May I help you?"

You will make the world a kinder and happier place and God will bless you.

Please Leave this World as You'd like to find it

Thought

I will do my part to make the world better.

September 20

Would not God have discovered it, since He knows the secrets of the heart?

Psalm 44:21

We may be able to keep a secret from our friends or even our parents but there are no secrets from God. He knows our every thought.

Slow to criticize

Quick to praise

Thought
I will think kind thoughts today.

September 21

... "If anyone wants to be first, he must be the very last, and the servant of all."

Mark 9:35

Ask an athlete "Who is the greatest?" He will say that the winner is the best. When Jesus was asked who was the greatest, he answered, "The person willing to serve others is greatest in God's eyes."

Thought
I want to be a winner in God's sight.

September 22

David said to Saul, "Let no one lose heart on account of this Philistine; your servant will go and fight him."
1 Samuel 17:32

Remember the Bible story of young David who killed the giant, Goliath, with his slingshot? How could a young boy do such a brave thing? He could do it because he believed in himself and believed, too, that God would help him.

WAS There ANYTHING you wanted to say to me, Sonny?

One minute while I fix this sling, Goliath.

Thought
Ask God to help you when you need to be strong and brave.

September 23

So we rebuilt the wall till all of it reached half its height, for the people worked with all their heart.

Nehemiah 4:6

When you are given a job to do, take the time to do it well. A sloppy, messy job will please no one, not even yourself.

I'm sure Jesus did his best in the carpenter shop with Joseph, His earthly father.

Thought
A job doing is worth doing well.

"Brighten the corner
where you are."

September 24

This is love for God; to obey his commands. And his commands are not burdensome, for everyone born of God overcomes the world.

1 John 5:3-4

It is easier to be a good person than a mean person.
When we choose to do what is right we live in harmony
with God and others.
Best of all, Christ is our helper.

Thought
Today I'm determined to do the right thing.

September 25

**These men are grumblers and faultfinders; they follow their own evil
desires; they boast about themselves and flatter others for
their own advantage.**

Jude 1:16

Do you know anyone who is a complainer? We all complain sometimes,
but nobody likes to listen to the person who is always unhappy
about something. Our heavenly Father waits
to hear our praise and thanksgiving.

Thought
When I whine and complain I disappoint
God who sends us His blessings so we will
enjoy our lives.

September 26

Though you have not seen him, you love him; and even though you do not see him now, you believe in him and are filled with an inexpressible and glorious joy,

1 Peter 1:8

A Christian has every reason to be filled with joy. Jesus showed each of us how much we are loved by God. He taught us the right way to live and promised us that we will live forever with Him in heaven.

Thought

Jesus fills my heart with joy.

September 27

Do not conform any longer to the pattern of this world, but be transformed by the renewing of your mind. Then you will be able to test and prove what God's will is– his good, pleasing and perfect will.

Romans 12:2

It's great to be popular, to have others friendship and approval, but not if it means that we must do what we know is not right.

Always choose God's approval above the approval of others.

Thought

God deserves first place
in my heart.

September 28

Jesus said, "It is more blessed to give than to receive."
Acts 20:35

Did you know that there is a right way to give and a wrong way to give?
The Bible tells us that God loves those who give cheerfully (2 Corinthians 9:7.)
Next time you give a friend a gift at a birthday
party, say a secret prayer for your friend. When you
pray for your friend to be happy, you'll find it's
easier to give your gift cheerfully.

And if you don't like the present, at least keep the smile

Thought
I am learning to be a cheerful giver.

September 29

"Come, follow me," Jesus said, "and I will make you fishers of men."

Matthew 4:19

Is there someone you look up to and admire? If so, that person is your hero.

Make sure that person deserves your admiration.

Ask yourself, "Is this a good person?"

If you have a younger brother or sister you may be the good example that little one will want to follow.

MY HERO

he can do up his shoe-laces.

Thought

I will try to be the best example

September 30

My guilt has overwhelmed me like a burden too heavy to bear.

Psalm 38:4

Each of us fails from time to time even after we have
done our very best.
In God's eyes our failure can be used for good.

Thought

If we make mistakes, God can use our mistakes
for good when we honor Him

October 1

"Don't be afraid!" David said to them, "for I will surely show you kindness for the sake of your father Jonathan. I will restore to you all the land that belongs to your grandfather Saul, and you will always eat at my table."

2 Samuel 9:7

David who killed the giant, Goliath, had a best friend named Jonathan. One day the two made a solemn promise or covenant to each other. They promised to be friends forever. Years later Jonathan was killed in a battle and David became king of Israel.
King David remembered his promise to Jonathan. When he learned that Jonathan had left behind a handicapped son, David invited him to live with him in his palace.

I will eat at Your table

Thought
Whatever I promise
I will do.

October 2

He gives strength to the weary and increases the power of the weak.
Isaiah 40:29

If you wait for everything to be just right before you do something that needs doing, that something may never get done. Do what you need to do, in rain or in sunshine, whether you are tired or rested, happy or sad.

Thought
I will not put off until tomorrow what
I must do today.

October 3

Surely goodness and loving kindness will follow me all the days of my life, and I will dwell in the house of the Lord forever.

Psalm 23:6

When you read your Bible often, pray to your heavenly Father and live by Christ's example you are growing strong in spirit. Remember, it's the spirit part of you that lives forever.

The Lord is my Guide-book

Thought
God's goodness and love are with me today.

October 4

And Jesus kept increasing in wisdom and stature, and in favor with God and men.

Luke 2:52

To grow in God's favor means to grow in God's approval.
Others in the Bible who grew up in God's favor were David,
Samuel, and Daniel, to name a few.
They all grew in favor by carefully doing God's will.

Thought

Each day I grow in favor with God and others.

October 5

Blessed are you when people insult you, persecute you, and falsely say all kind of evil against you because of me.

Matthew 5:11

Joan refused to go along with her friends and tease the new girl on the block. "You are a 'goody-two shoes", they jeered.

When others make fun of you because you are kind, Jesus says be happy about it. God is pleased and will reward you.

Thought

I will do the right thing no matter what.

October 6

In the same way, let your light shine before men, that they may see your good deeds and praise your Father in heaven.

Matthew 5:16

Think of yourself today
as a candle burning brightly.
Light up someone's day by a smile or a kind word.

Thought
This little light of mine, I will let it shine.

October 7

Then Jacob gave Esau bread and some lentil stew. He ate and drank and then got up and left. So Esau despised his birthright.

Genesis 25:34

Esau and Jacob were brothers. Esau cared more about food and eating than he cared about God. Jacob was not perfect, but he wanted God's blessing above everything. God blessed Jacob for this.

Just as I am, please bless me.

Thought

Nothing is worth more than God's blessing.

October 8

...because the Lord disciplines those he loves, as a father the son he delights in.

Proverbs 3:12

From time to time each of us needs to be corrected. How else can we learn if someone doesn't tell us when we are wrong?
Be grateful for correction even though you may not be glad to have your mistakes pointed out. When you are willing to learn from your mistakes, you show that you are wise.

Thought
I will be wise and learn from my mistakes.

October 9

The heavens declare the glory of God; the skied proclaim the work of his hands.

Psalm 19:1

Twinkle, twinkle little star
How I wonder what you are.
Up above the world so high,
Like a diamond in the sky.

Some things talk best
by just shining.

Thought

The beauty of the starry night reminds me of God.

October 10

God is our refuge and strength, an ever-present help in trouble.
Psalm 46:1

When you have a problem, try to figure out a solution.
Perhaps someone may be able to help you.

And God's help is there for you
when you ask him for it.

Please
—
Drop in for
a prayer
any time

Thought
God is bigger than my problem.

October 11

May the words of my mouth and the meditation of my heart be pleasing in your sight, O Lord, my Rock and My Redeemer.

Psalm 19:14

Do you know how important our thoughts are? The person who is kind to others first thought a kind thought. The unkind person first had unkind thoughts. Notice what you are thinking. Choose to let good thoughts lead you.

Thought

Today I will do my best to think good thoughts.

October 12

But everyone who hears these words of mine and does not put them into practice is like a foolish man who built his house on sand.

Matthew 7:26

Have you ever built a sand castle at the beach and had it swept away by the sea?

Jesus tells us to be wise and follow his teachings;

so that when big waves of trouble come we will be strong and safe.

Thought

I have decided to follow Jesus.

WITH JESUS ALONE

October 13

You will pray to him and he will hear you, and you will fulfill all your vows.

Job 22:27

Our Father hears us when we pray,

A whisper He can hear.

He know not only what we say,

But what we wish or fear.

Thought

God hears my every prayer.

October 14

Trust in the Lord with all your heart and lean not on your own understanding;

Proverbs 3:5

Most children like to ask questions that begin with the word, "Why?"

Even adults often ask "Why?" questions. Some of our questions have no answers. For example, we always ask, "Why do bad things sometimes happen to good people?" That is a question that only God can answer.

Thought

When I don't have an answer, I simply trust God.

But why, Lord

October 15

For I am the Lord, your God, who takes hold of your right hand and say to you, Do not fear; I will help you.

Isaiah 41:13

When I am weak, God is strong.
When I am shy and timid, God says, "Fear Not."
When I am tempted to do wrong, God strengthens me.

I Listen to your voice

Thought
With God I am strong and unafraid.

October 16

And he (Jesus) took the children in his arms, put his hands on them and blessed them.

Mark 10:16

Jesus always has
the last word

Jesus, Friend of little children
Be a friend to me.
Take my hand, and ever keep me close to Thee.
Teach me how to grow in goodness
Daily as I grow.
You have been a child, and surely You do know.
Never leave me or forsake me,
Ever be my friend,
For I need you from life's dawning to its end.
-W.J. Mathams

Thought
Thank you, Jesus, for being my friend!

October 17

Be strong and courageous, because you will lead these people to inherit the land I swore to their forefathers to give them.

Joshua 1:6

God's Top Ten List
Don't have any other gods.
Don't make or worship idols.
Don't misuse God's name.
Remember the Lord's Day.
Honor your father and mother.
Don't murder.
Don't commit adultery.
Don't steal.
Don't talk against your neighbor.
Don't be envious of your neighbor.

Thought
I will remember to obey God's commands.

October 18

Everyone who competes in the games goes into strict training. They do it to get a crown that will not last; but we do it to get a crown that will last forever.

1 Corinthians 9:25

Get it away from me if you can.

Games are fun but in almost every game there is a winner and a loser. Sometimes you win, sometimes you lose. When you are the winner, be happy about it, but don't strut around like a proud bird. When you are the loser, try to be a good sport and say something nice to the winner.

To play your best is truly more important than winning or losing.

Thought
Win or lose, I will be a good sport.

October 19

The Lord appeared to us in the past saying, "I have loved you with an everlasting love; I have drawn you with loving-kindness."
Jeremiah 31:3

What is it that makes a person important? It is not the person's age, size, looks, talents or even his or her actions. Each of us is important because God created us, loves us, and has given us our spirits that live forever.

Remember, everyone is important
to our heavenly Father.

but Jesus doesn't mind
when I get Muddy feet.

Thought
Each person is important in God's eyes.

October 20

For you have been my hope, O Sovereign Lord, my confidence since my youth.

Psalm 71:5

One reason children are so special to God is that they trust and believe in him with all their heart.

Thought
I have great hope because
God keeps His word.

October 21

Even the youths grow tired and weary, and young men stumble and fall; but those who hope in the Lord will renew their strength. They shall soar on wings like eagles; they will run and not be weary; they shall walk and not faint.

Isaiah 40:30-31

When you feel tired of trying and would like to give up think of the scripture that promises new strength for those who wait for the Lord.

And how does one wait for the Lord?

My discipline is our two daily walks.

By asking for His strength and by being thankful for the strength God sends.

Thought

Jesus gives me the strength I need for every task.

October 22

Search me, O God, and know my heart; test me and know my anxious thoughts.

Psalm 139:23

Search, try, O God, my thoughts and heart,
If mischief lurks in any part,
Correct me where I go astray
And guide me in Your perfect way.

Thought
When God corrects me it is
proof of His love.

If there's a way down, there's a way up.

WAY DOWN

October 23

Jesus turned and saw her. "Take heart, daughter," he said, "your faith has healed you." And the woman was healed from that moment.

Matthew 9:22

Everywhere Jesus went He saw people who needed one of His healing miracles. Those who believed in His power to heal received healing.

Little girl, I say unto you, arise

Thought

God's healing miracles happen every day.

October 24

Dear friends, let us love one another, for love comes from God. Everyone who loves has been born of God and knows God.

1 John 4:7

Friends come in all ages, sizes and colors. Each has his or her special personality. A friend is a lovable person who returns your love.

Thought
I'm thankful for each of my friends.

October 25

Arise, shine, for your light has come, and the glory of the Lord rises upon you.

Isaiah 60:1

Next time you are in church notice the
beautiful stained glass windows.
The colors look dark until the sunlight shines through.
When we live in loving kindness,
we are like glowing windows
bringing joy to all who see us.

Thought

Lord, may Your love shine through me today.

October 26

To these four young men God gave knowledge and understanding of all kinds of literature and learning. And David could understand visions and dreams of all kinds!

Daniel 1:17

God gives to each of us special talents and abilities.
God wants us to use these gifts
and talents to honor him.

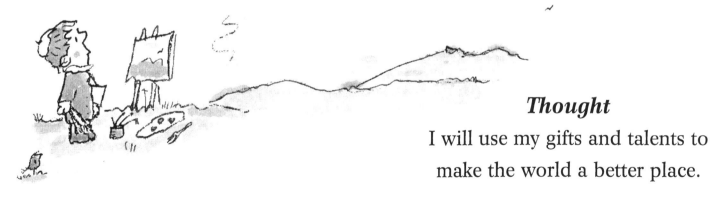

Thought

I will use my gifts and talents to
make the world a better place.

October 27

And the Lord replied, "My presence will go with you, and I will give you rest."

Exodus 33:14

One of the U.S. presidents, Dwight D. Eisenhower, used this favorite hymn in his prayer time:

I need You every hour
Most gracious Lord.
No tender voice like Thine can peace afford.
I need You, O I need You,
Every hour I need You.
O bless me now, my Savior – I come to You.

Thought

Lord, I need You every hour to help me be my very best.

October 28

The fear of the Lord is the beginning of knowledge, but fools despise wisdom and discipline.

Proverbs 1:7

What is true wisdom? It is simply to know what is right and to do it.

Thought

Thank you God, for teaching me right from wrong.

Your word is a guide to my paths.

October 29

My son, do not despise the Lord's discipline and do not resent his rebuke, because the Lord disciplines those he loves, just as a father the son he delights in.

Proverbs 3:11

How do you act when you've asked permission to go some place or do something you really wanted to do and the answer was, "No, you cannot do that"?

Do you beg, argue and whine?

Stop. Think.

"Who is in charge?

Who knows best?"

Thought

I will accept "No" for an answer without making a scene.

October 30

Do not be anxious about anything; but in everything, by prayer and petition with thanksgiving, present your requests to God.

Philippians 4:6

I get so worried about Mount Everest, I can't climb the hill next door

A "worry wart" is afraid and fearful.
The "worry wart" has forgotten that God
never slumbers or sleeps.
He will take care of us.

Thought
I have nothing to dread or fear.
God is in charge.

October 31

You will not fear the terror of night, nor the arrow that flies by day.
Psalm 91:5

Do the spooky Halloween costumes and masks make you feel afraid?
If you feel afraid, put your hand in the hand
of your friend or your parent
and laugh at the goblins.

Thought
I feel safe and protected with those I love.

November 1

Give thanks to the Lord, call upon his name; make known among the nations what he has done.

1 Chronicles 16:8

Did you know that we give thanks to God by what we do as well as by what we say? When you are cheerful, when things aren't going your way, when you are willing to share, when you take care of your things – these actions say a loud, clear "Thank You" to God.

Thought
I will thank God by my actions.

November 2

"Be careful not to do your acts of righteousness before men, to be seen by them. If you do you will have no reward from your Father in heaven."

Matthew 6:1

Watch out for hypocrites!
Hypocrites pretend to be so holy and good, but they mainly want praise and compliments.
Jesus knew who really loved God and who were only pretending to love Him.

Thought
I don't want to be a hypocrite or a show off.
I want to truly love.

November 3

Your kingdom is an everlasting kingdom, and your dominion endures through all generations.

Psalm 145:13

When we pray the Lord's Prayer we pray, "May Your Kingdom come." What is this kingdom we are praying for? It's the Kingdom that Jesus showed us—a kingdom of love, light, joy, peace and goodness that never ends. It's a kingdom we can enter when we trust Christ and live as He taught us.

Thought
I live happily in the goodness of God's kingdom.

November 4

**"Ah, Sovereign Lord," I said , "I do not know how to speak;
I am only a child."**

Jeremiah 1:6

Never believe just because you're young that you can't be of great value to God's Kingdom. The Bible is full of examples of young people God began preparing for a great work He had in mind for them. One example is Esther, a young woman who saved her people from evil men. And who could forget David, the young shepherd boy who killed the giant, or the young boy offering his two loaves and fishes that Jesus used to feed thousands of people?

Thought
I'm not too young to be useful in God's Kingdom.

November 5

It is good to praise the Lord, and make music to your name, O Most High.

Psalm 92:1

Thought

I will sing a song of praise to the Lord today for all His blessings.

We plow the fields and scatter
The good seeds on the land.
But it is fed and watered
By God's almighty hand.
He sends the snow in winter,
The warmth to swell the grain,
The breezes and the sunshine,
And soft refreshing rain.
All good gifts around us
Are sent from heaven above.
Then thank the Lord, O thank
The Lord for all His love.

– *Malthias Claudum*

November 6

Enter his gates with thanksgiving and his courts with praise, give thanks to him to praise his name.

Psalm 100:4

A sincere "thank you" pleases your heavenly Father.

Besides at mealtime and bedtime, can you remember to pause and say "thank you" to God for a special blessing today?

Merci   Gratias

Danke

Woof   Thank
You

Many voices
one meaning

Thought
I will make thanksgiving a habit.

November 7

The earth is the Lord's, and everything in it, the world and all who live in it, . . .

Psalm 24:1

Look around you. Notice the beauty everywhere that God has made. Name some of the beautiful things you can see out your window.

Thought

God fills His world with beauty

November 8

I will give thanks to the Lord because of his righteousness and will sing praise to the name of the Lord most High.

Psalm 7:17

Can you think of some of the names of our Lord God? When we think of all creation he has made, we call him the _____ (creator). When we think of his great power we call him the Almighty _____ (King). When we think of Jesus who died on the cross for our sins, we call his name _____ (Savior).

Thought

God is awesome. Who could ever praise Him enough?

November 9

"Now then my son, listen to me; blessed are those who keep my ways."

Proverbs 8:32

Thought

Day by day in every
way I am learning
how to live happily.

It takes a lifetime to learn how to live,
How to share and how to give.
How to find courage to face each day,
How to face tragedy that comes your way.
How to smile when your heart is sore,
How to go on when you can take no more.
How to laugh when you want to cry,
How to be brave when you say good-bye.
How to forgive when your urge is to hate,
How to be sure that God is really there.
How to find Him—Seek Him in prayer.

– Tena Fortenberry

November 10

Sing for joy to God our strength; shout aloud to the God of Jacob.

Psalms 81:1

When you awakened this morning, did you feel full of
energy, ready to play and have fun?
Your strong and healthy body is a special blessing from God.

Thought

I am thankful that I am healthy
and full of energy.

November 11

**I will praise the Lord, who counsels me; even at night
my heart instructs me.**

Psalm 16:7

What should I do? What should I say?
Which way should I go?
When questions puzzle you, turn to the
Lord and ask His advice.
Quietly wait
for His direction.

Thought

Nothing is too small or too difficult
to ask God.

November 12

Blessed is the nation whose God is the Lord, the people he chose for his inheritance.

Psalm 33:12

The United States government is a government of laws. On the coins and bills you can see the words "In God We Trust". Lawmakers in congress begin their work with an opening prayer.

The government exists to protect and serve the people.

Dear Lord.
please bless
America.

Thought

God has blessed America with peace and wealth.

November 13

I will extol the Lord at all times; his praise will always be on my lips.

Psalm 34:1

It's easy to be thankful when all's going well and everything
is going our way. Times when we are hurt or disappointed it
is harder to praise, but good things begin to happen when we
choose to be thankful even when things go wrong.

Thought

Even when I am sad, I can find something
I'm thankful for.

November 14

**Be imitators of God, therefore, as dearly loved children and
live a life of love...**

Ephesians 5:1

Children are good at imitating. How can you be an imitator of God today?
Think Godly thoughts, speak words of truth and kindness and live as you
believe Jesus would live.

close attention

Thought
I will imitate my heavenly Father today.

November 15

"I have loved you with an ever lasting love..."
Jeremiah 31: 3

Even the little birds find rest in my branches

We can only see a little of God's loving,
A few rich treasures from His mighty store;
But out there – beyond, beyond our eyes horizon,
There's more – there's more.
– *Anonymous*

Thought
I cannot measure God's love for me.

November 16

A righteous man may have many troubles, but the Lord delivers him from them all.

Psalms 34:19

Yes, bad things sometimes happen to good people. Even so, in the worst times the good person chooses to love God, trust Him, and stay thankful.

Thought
God will help me when trouble comes my way.

November 17

Be still before the Lord and wait patiently for him,...

Psalms 37:7

Sometimes the hardest thing to do is wait.
Someone said, "God is
never early, but He is never late."
Growing up takes a long time.
While growing in God's ways, expect
great blessings.

I wait for your love.

Thought

I will wait patiently for God's rewards.

November 18

You have made known to me the path of life; you will fill me with joy in your presence,...

Psalms 16:11

Childrens' faces, and your face, reflect the glory of the Lord. That is why children are greatly loved. The sight of your face, because it reflects God's Spirit inside you, can bring great joy to others, especially to those who are very old and lonely.

Do you know an older person you could cheer up?

Thought

I am grateful for God's spirit within me.

November 19

I press on toward the goal to win the prize for which God has called me heavenward in Christ Jesus.

Philippians 3:14

There is no thrill quite like doing something you didn't know you could. I never knew I could create a beautiful picture worthy of framing until I took art lessons.

Be willing to try something even when it seems too hard for you. You might even surprise yourself.

Reaching for a better world

Thought
I will set big goals because God Himself
is my helper.

November 20

A friend loves at all times.

Proverbs 17:17

A loving friend can love enough to forgive, to share,
to listen, and help.
Can you think of other ways to be a good friend?

Thought

I will love my friend even when he (or she) acts unlovable.

November 21

Why are you so downcast, O my soul? Why so disturbed within me? Put your hope in God, for I will yet praise him; my Savior and my God.

Psalms 43:5

Think of God as your invisible friend.
He is always with you, guiding
you, and willing to help you when you ask
Him in simple trust.

Thought
God's love puts a smile on my face.

November 22

I can do everything through him who gives me strength.

Philippians 4:13

When life throws you a curve ball, HIT IT!

Or practice making a

great catch.

Life is the biggest
Curveball of all

Thought

I will see problems today as ways to let
my faith and abilities stretch and grow.

November 23

Stop judging by mere appearances, and make a right judgment.
John 7:24

There's a well-known saying that says, "You can't judge a book by its cover." To really know whether you will like the book you have to open it and have a look inside. It's the same with people. By just looking at their faces, their clothes or their skin color we can't know what the person is truly like until we get to know them.

Thought
It takes time to get to know someone.

November 24

It is good to praise the Lord, and make music to your name, O Most High; to proclaim your love in the morning and your faithfulness at night.

Psalms 92:1-2

Sun and rain,
Work and play,
Grant to us, Lord,
day by day.

Today is a good day to name the things in your life that you are thankful for. After you have named these things remember that all we have comes from God. God expects His children to give Him thanks.

Thought
Every day brings a shower of blessings.

November 25

Great is the Lord, and most worthy of praise.
Psalms 48:1

When you say "thank you" to God it's important to truly mean it. Don't pray like a parrot – a lot of words but with no feeling. And make sure you are a promise keeper, just as God himself keeps His promises without fail.

Pouring from a full heart

Thought
I will give God my heartfelt praise.

November 26

"In everything I did, I showed you that by this kind of hard work we must help the weak, remembering the words of Lord Jesus himself said: 'It is more blessed to give than to receive.' "

Acts 20:35

Which is more fun, to give a gift or get a gift? Most would say it's more fun to get a gift, but Jesus says that it is a happier thing to give than to get. As you grow up in God's kingdom and become more and more loving you will understand more about the joy of giving.

Thought
I am learning to be a joyful giver.

November 27

From heaven the Lord looks down and sees all mankind; from his dwelling place he watches all who live on earth.

Psalms 33:13-15

Knowing that God, our heavenly Father, watches each one of us and knows everything we do is something to be glad about.

The only time God's watchfulness disturbs us is when we are not living as He taught us.

Thought
I will live everyday in a way
that is pleasing to God.

November 28

"...but whoever listens to me will live in safety and be at ease; without fear of harm."

Proverbs 1:33

As God's children we are not to worry. It is one of God's great "DO NOTS". Wanting our own way causes all our fretting and worrying. By keeping our minds on God's will and not our own we can be spared the misery of worry.

Jesus' purpose was not to please himself but to fulfill His Father's plans. Jesus never worried or fretted.

You love me when the waves rise higher

Thought

With God in charge I need not worry.

November 29

The light shines in the darkness but the darkness has not understood it.

John 1:5

It is strange, Lord
the effect of a candle:
so trivial a thing,
so small a piece of wax.
And yet I light it,
and for a little space
the darkness is driven back,
so that the world itself is lighter
because of my candle,
because of my one good deed,
because of my one life.
— *Graham Jeffery*

Reaching
the switch

LOVE

Thought
I will light up someone's life
today with kindness.

November 30

We give thanks to you, O God, we give thanks for your Name is near; men tell of your wonderful deeds.

Psalms 75:1

God's miracles are everywhere.
Each sunrise is a miracle, each newborn
Baby and even each leaf and each flower.

Thought

I will be on the lookout
for God's miracles today.

December 1

But the angel said to her, "Do not be afraid, Mary, you have found
favor with God. You will be with child and give birth to a son,
and you are to give him the name Jesus."
Luke 1:30-31

It will soon be time to get ready for Christmas! Is your Christmas list ready?
In the stores Christmas decorations are everywhere.

It's the biggest holiday celebration of the year.

Whose birthday are we celebrating?

How do you think Jesus likes us to celebrate

His birthday?

Thought
I will remember it is Jesus' birthday.

December 2

Mary said, 'May it be to me as you have said." Then the angel left her.
Luke 1:38

Before Jesus was born an angel spoke to His Mother, Mary, telling her she would give birth to the Savior of the world who would be Christ, the Lord. Turn in your Bible to Luke 1:46-55 for Mary's words in response to the angel's announcement. Mary quietly and calmly made preparations for this great event to happen.

Here am I, send me.

Thought
I, too, am preparing my heart for Christmas.

December 3

...and she gave birth to her firstborn, a son. She wrapped him in cloths and placed him in a manger because there was no room for them in the inn.

Luke 2:7

No room! No room in the inn for Jesus Christ, God's only Son,
born to save the world? Years later the innkeeper may have sighed,
"If only I had known!"
Each one of us is the innkeeper of our heart.
May the Lord Jesus find a welcome place there.

Thought
I will make room for Jesus in my heart.

December 4

Then my enemy will see it and will be covered with shame, she who said to me, "Where is the Lord your God?" My eyes will see her downfall; even now she will be trampled underfoot like mire in the streets.

Micah 7:10

Winners and losers, losers and winners – that's how people are often labeled in our daily lives. In God's eyes, however, He never sees us as losers. When we love and serve Him we are on His team, the winning team, never the losing team.

Thought

I'm glad to be on God's winning team.

December 5

"...Peace, peace, to those far and near," says the Lord.

"And I will heal them."

Isaiah 57:19

The shepherds heard the angels sing the night Jesus was born.

They sang, "Glory to God, and on earth peace among men." (Luke 2:14)

On many of our Christmas cards the message is often the same,

"Peace on earth, good will to men."

How can you and I spread peace in the world?

It could be as easy as giving someone a smile.

Thought

How silently, how silently the gift of peace is given.

December 6

"This will be a sign to you: You will find a baby wrapped in cloths and lying in a Manger."

Luke 2:12

Away in a manger, no crib for a bed,
The little Lord Jesus laid down His sweet head.
The stars in the bright sky looked down where He lay,
The little Lord Jesus asleep on the hay.
The cattle are lowing the Baby awakes,
But little Lord Jesus no crying He makes.
I love Thee, Lord Jesus, look down from the sky,
And stay by my side until morning is nigh.
Be near me, Lord Jesus, I ask Thee to stay
Close by me forever, and love me, I pray.
Bless all the dear children in Thy tender care,
And fit us for heaven to live with Thee there. Amen

I wonder what this child will be ..?

Thought
A manger filled with hay was Jesus' first bed.

December 7

My dear brothers, take note of this: Everyone should be quick to listen, slow to speak and slow to become angry,...

James 1:19

By the way you speak to parents, teachers, and older people you show them your respect. By answering when you are spoken to rather than just turning away, and by trying to remember not to interrupt, you are showing your thoughtfulness.

Thought
The best speech is thoughtful speech.

December 8

Nothing in all creation is hidden from God's sight...
Hebrews 4:13

Have you ever heard the saying,
"There's a little watch-bird watching you?"
I'm not sure what a watch-bird is, but I am sure that
someone is watching each one of us every day.
How do people see you? How does God see you?
People judge us by how we behave. God judges us by
the thoughts of our hearts.

Thought
I want my thoughts, words, and actions to please my Father in heaven.

December 9

**And Jesus grew in wisdom and stature,
and in favor with God and men.**

Luke 2:52

Height   Favor

Growing up is a two-way
process

Thought

I will be friendly to everyone I meet today.

At work beside His father's bench,
At play when work was done,
In quiet Galilee He lived,
The friend of everyone.
Friend of boys and girls like us,
Playmate so straight and true,
In all our work, in all our play,
Make us friends like you.
And as He grew to be a man
He wandered far and wide,
To be a friend to all in need
Throughout the countryside.
Friend of men, so strong and true,
Help us strong friends to be,
Make of us true friends one and all,
To others and to Thee.
– Alice M. Pullen

December 10

So they hurried off and found Mary and Joseph, and the baby who was lying in the manger.

Luke 2:16

Today is a good day to get out the manger scene that our family has treasured for years. The stable is made of cardboard but the other pieces are pottery. The pieces of hay which we sprinkle around reminds us that Jesus was not born in a golden palace but in a barn with the farm animals. He made His home with the meek and lowly while here on earth.

Thought
The baby in the manger was born to be the Savior of the world.

December 11

For this God is our God for ever and ever; he will be our guide even to the end.

Psalm 48:14

Father, lead me day by day;
Ever in Your own sweet way;
Teach me to be pure and true;
Show me what I ought to do.
– John Page Hopps

Jesus takes me for the best walks

Thought
Wherever God leads me I will follow.

December 12

After Jesus has said this, he went on ahead going up to Jerusalem.
Luke 19:28

Someday I hope to visit the land of Jesus' birth. I would like to see Bethlehem, Nazareth and Jerusalem. The places would all be greatly changed after two thousand years, but I know the empty tomb where Jesus rose from the dead is still there. And all of us believers have His parting promise, "Lo, I am with you always, even until the end of the world."

Thought
The Holy Land is the place where Jesus lived on earth, but His Spirit is with us here and now.

December 13

This is to my Father's glory, that you bear much fruit, showing yourselves to be my disciples.

John 15:8

Do dandelions grow in your yard? Have you ever picked a bouquet of dandelions? Some people think dandelions are just weeds, but I think they can teach us some valuable lessons. The dandelion grows and blooms in some of the toughest places—even from cracks in sidewalks.

Watering the plant of LIFE.

They never fail to bloom and their seeds blow everywhere.

Thought
I will bloom where I am planted.

December 14

On coming to the house, they saw the child with his mother Mary, and they bowed down and worshiped him. Then they opened their treasures and presented him with gifts of gold, incense and myrrh.

Matthew 2:11

Christmas shoppers hurry to and fro
Looking for treasures their loved ones to show.
While carols ring and voices sing
Christians seek to honor their King.
With their gifts for others, given in love,
Christ is honored on earth and in heaven above.

Thought

God loves a cheerful giver.

December 15

"I am the good shepherd.
The good shepherd lays down his life for the sheep."
John 10:11

Jesus called Himself the Good Shepherd. He called us, His followers, His sheep.
The Christmas candy cane is shaped like a shepherd's crook.
Let it remind you of Jesus, our Good Shepherd.

Thought
The Lord leads me like a shepherd.

December 16

He tends his flock like a shepherd: he gathers the lambs in his arms and carries them close to have heart: he gently leads those who have young.

Isaiah 40:11

Because the Lord is my Shepherd, I have everything I need. He lets me rest in the meadow grass, and leads me beside the quiet streams. He restores my failing health. He helps me to do what honors Him the most. Even when walking through the dark valley of death I will not be afraid, for You are close beside me, guarding, guiding all the way. You provide delicious food for me in the presence of my enemies. You have welcomed me as your guest; blessings overflow. Your goodness and unfailing kindness shall be with me all of my life, and afterwards I will live forever with You in Your home. The Good Shepherd's Psalm

Thought
I am one of Jesus' lambs.

December 17

After they had heard the king, they went on their way, and the star seen in the east went ahead of them until it stopped over the place where the child was.

Matthew 2:9

What things at Christmastime remind you of Jesus? I'm reminded of Jesus when I see a manger scene and when I see the star on top of a Christmas tree like the star that the wise men followed.

Thought

The wise men brought gifts to baby Jesus of gold, frankincense and myrrh.

December 18

And the child grew and become strong; he was filled with wisdom, and the grace of God was upon him.

Luke 2:40

It takes a long time for a baby to become a grown-up. It takes a long time for the seed that is planted to become a tree. Each one of us is slowly growing and becoming the person God would have us to be.

Thought
God isn't finished with me yet.

December 19

He guides the humble in what is right and teaches them his way.

Psalm 25:9

We have God's book, the Bible, His church and people who are good Christian examples to teach and guide us.

and I follow in Jesus' footsteps

Thought

God's ways are the best ways.

as best I may

December 20

For God so loved the world that he gave his one and only Son, that whoever believes in him shall not perish, but have eternal life.

John 3:16

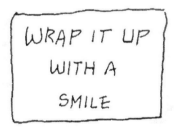

Christmastime is gift giving time. Each gift we so carefully choose, wrap and give is a way we show our love. God showed His great love for us by giving us His only Son, Jesus Christ, on the very first Christmas.

Thought

The best gifts are tied with heartstrings.

December 21

And now these three remain: faith, hope and love.

But the greatest of these is love.

1 Corinthians 13:13

Thought
Others will know I'm a
Christian by my love.

Love came down at Christmas
Love all lovely, Love divine;
Love was born at Christmas,
Star and angels gave the sign.
Love shall be our offering,
Love be yours and Love be mine,
Love to God and all men
Love our plea, our gift, our sign.
– *Christina Rossetti*

December 22

I have told you this so that my joy may be in you and your joy may be complete.

John 15:11

The Christian author, C.S. Lewis, wrote a book called *Surprised by Joy.*

Does it surprise you to know that the joy you feel at Christmastime can be yours all year long as you follow Jesus?

Thought

The Lord keeps surprising me with joy when I follow Him.

December 23

You have filled my heart with greater joy than when their grain and new wine abound.

Psalm 4:7

Can you can hardly wait until Christmas? What fun it will be to open our gifts that are under the tree. Jesus was given gifts of gold, frankincense, and myrrh by the wise men that saw His star and followed it to the manger.

The whole world had been waiting for long years for the King God had promised to be born.

No wonder the angels sang,

"Joy to the World."

Thought

I am full of joy today.

December 24

Every good and perfect gift is from above, coming down from the Father of the heavenly lights, who does not change like shifting shadows.

James 1:17

Twas the night before Christmas, when all through the house
Not a creature was stirring—not even a mouse.
The stockings were hung by the chimney with care.
In hopes that St. Nicholas soon would be there."

What is it that makes St. Nicholas or Santa Claus so special? Why, all the gifts he gives us, of course! Tonight as you think about the gifts you hope for, remember baby Jesus—God's gift to you and to me and to the whole world.

Thought

God gave Jesus to be the Savior of the world.

December 25

He will be a joy and delight to you, and many will rejoice because of his birth.

Luke 1:14

Jesus Christ is born today! Hallelujah!
Songs of praise then let us sing Unto
Christ our heavenly King.
Sing we to our God above Praise as
lasting as His love. Hallelujah!

Jesus is very particular
who he visits

Thought

The day of Jesus' birth brings joy and gladness.

December 26

If you obey my commands, you will remain in my love, just as I have obeyed my Father's commands and remain in his love.

John 15:10

What are the gifts you bring to the King?
I offer Him worship, His praises I sing.
What can I offer from my treasure?
I can offer Him love without measure.
Only my best gifts are fit for the King.
I give Him my heart, my everything.

Thought
Love and obedience are gifts I offer to Jesus my King.

December 27

I will sing to the Lord, because he has been good to me.

Psalm 13:6

It will soon be time to pack away the Christmas decorations. Our lives must get back to our normal routine. The best part of Christmas, however, can be with us each day. Choose to keep the happiness, the peace, the love, and the gladness of Christmas in your thoughts and actions.

Thought

I will celebrate every day.

God loves to hear his crows as well as his nightingales.

December 28

Who may ascend the hill of the Lord? Who may stand in his holy place? He who has clean hands and a pure heart, who does not lift up his soul to an idol or swear by what is false.

Psalm 24:3-4

People who are mean, selfish, unkind, and untruthful do not live in the Lord's presence. An evil spirit leads them. They will never know God's peace and joy until they change their ways.

Its only me. Lord

Thought
I want to be pure and honest.

December 29

Wait for the Lord; be strong and take heart and wait for the Lord.

Psalm 27:14

Waiting is hard but God is never in a hurry. As one person said,
"God's blessings are always on time, but never early."

I'm still here, Lord

Thought

I will be patient while I wait for God's answers.

December 30

When Jesus spoke again to the people, he said, "I am the light of the world. Whoever follows me will never walk in darkness, but will have the light of life."

John 8:12

Thought

The Bible is all about Jesus.

God has given us a book full of stories,
Which was made for His people of old,
It begins with the tale of a garden,
And ends with the city of God.
But the best is the story of Jesus,
Of the babe and the ox in the stall,
Of the song that was sung by the angels,
The most beautiful story of all.
There are stories for parents and children,
For the old who are ready to rest,
But for all who can read them or listen,
The story of Jesus is best;
For it tells how He came from the Father,
His far-away children to call,
To bring the lost sheep to their Shepherd,
The most beautiful story of all.

– Maria M. Penstone

December 31

"I am the Alpha and the Omega," says the Lord God, "who is and who was, and who is to come, the Almighty."

Revelations 1:8

Today is a special day to celebrate. It is New Year's Eve, the very last day of the old year. Many people will celebrate with parties to welcome the New Year. Not one of us knows what the New Year may bring, but we do know that God is in charge and His Kingdom is on its way. Happy New Year!

Thought
Only God knows the past,
present and future.

The end of one year is the beginning of another.

Made in the USA
Charleston, SC
16 August 2012